LIVE WIRES

'Dan Warner's intimately experiential/technical descriptions of his favorite instances of every kind and genre of electronic music in the experimental culture – a culture that almost obliterated the boundaries between "classical" and "pop" – will get you right inside of his sensitively perceptive ear and his deep knowledge and understanding of the sense and implication of what he has, and you will, come to hear.'
– Benjamin Boretz, composer

'The key to success with a book of this type is balance; too much detail and the layman is left baffled, but too little leaves more informed readers with a craving for chewy morsels of depth. Where authors such as Simon Reynolds employed a sociological approach in *Energy Flash* and David Toop's *Ocean of Sound* was one of philosophy, Daniel Warner examines technology in order to analyse the music . . . Where descriptive sections could have been burdened with the dryness of unnecessary academic heft, they are lightened here by an authorial style that indicates a love of the music alongside a wealth of knowledge. Definitely best consumed whilst imbibing his excellent chapter of recommended listening.' – *Shindig!*

'Warner gives us just enough theory to grasp the significance of each development or key work. It's a good introduction to the artistic aims and means of an ever-expanding sound world, and – from Varèse to Blondie to Squarepusher to DJ Shadow – makes for an invigorating and nostalgic playlist.' – *BBC Music Magazine*

'The writing is easy to read, knowledgeable without being painfully esoteric. A remarkable Recommended Listening appendix should keep us all busy for at least a decade to come . . . We are merely passengers on this intellectually stimulating and frequently entertaining ride . . . This is a wonderful guide through a still-evolving phenomenon and one that now, more than ever, deserves our attention.' – *Spectrum Culture*

'Music has long been part of our sonic soundscape. But, beginning in the 1950s and continuing through to current day, seemingly endless combinations of new technologies and creative endeavors created experimental electronic music. *Live Wires* captures that synergy with engaging history and personal insights . . . Those readers with some awareness of the background Warner provides will find the story engaging. Those with no history with electronic music will find it a sonic adventure well worth reading.' – *Leonardo*

'*Live Wires* rips open the term to tell the wider story of the how those tapes and wires and transistors came to transform music into what we take for granted today . . . Warner starts with the earliest sound manipulators cutting up and slowing down tapes and zigzags his way to the present day where a laptop is that mainstay of many a performance artist.' – Popmatters.com

'If we dare mention Christmas, this book would make a perfect stocking filler for Electronica fans . . . oh, right. Yes, that's you. Self-gift?' – *Electrowow*

'There are big books, and little books. Books that are large because they collect myriad examples of "the exact thing you need to know" about a given subject – the volume to which you have gone a hundred times for a hundred different answers. But there are also volumes that, like the Tardis, are bigger on the inside – books that read well, make their point, and then send you elsewhere – they encapsulate how you think of something. Books you circle around and back to as you continue to chase down the ideas they contain. Daniel Warner's *Live Wires* is one of those books . . . I commend this book to your attention.' – Cycling '74

'Useful as a primer to those interested in learning more about this fascinating – and still mysterious – sonic landscape.' – 4Columns.org

LIVE WIRES

A HISTORY OF ELECTRONIC MUSIC

DANIEL WARNER

REAKTION BOOKS

This book is dedicated to the memory of David Cook Morse who, on a cold winter's day in 1970, played two records for me: Béla Bartók playing selections from his Mikrokosmos *and King Crimson's* In the Court of the Crimson King

Published by Reaktion Books Ltd
Unit 32, Waterside
44–48 Wharf Road
London N1 7UX, UK

www.reaktionbooks.co.uk

First published 2017
First published in paperback 2019
Copyright © Daniel Warner 2017

Printed and bound in Great Britain
by Bell & Bain, Glasgow

A catalogue record for this book is available from the British Library

ISBN 978 1 78914 141 2

CONTENTS

INTRODUCTION 7
1 TAPE RECORDER 17
2 CIRCUITS 55
3 TURNTABLE AND RECORD 89
4 MICROPHONE 111
5 COMPUTERS 131
EPILOGUE 170

RECOMMENDED LISTENING 173
REFERENCES 181
BIBLIOGRAPHY 191
ACKNOWLEDGEMENTS 195
PHOTO ACKNOWLEDGEMENTS 197
INDEX 199

Eurorack format analogue synthesizer.

INTRODUCTION

This book tries to catch the exciting synergy between new and still emerging musical forms and rapidly changing technologies. To address the challenges of representing one of the significant cultural shifts of the last century and into our own, while at the same time doing justice to the open-endedness and potentialities of a new audio culture, has meant accepting and embracing the discontinuities of discovery, reflection and materiality that would constitute a new electronic music history.

Walter Benjamin famously argued in his essay on art and technology that 'mechanical reproduction' changed the relationship between the 'work of art' and cultural value.[1] For him, the mechanical reproduction of works of art caused a certain loss of their 'aura' and meaningfulness. Nowhere is this problem more crucial than in the reproduction and creation of sound. Nearly a century later, the debates around what is art and especially what is music are still unresolved. What is undeniable is that the astounding contributions and collaborations of musicians and engineers have made room for a much more inclusive and democratic approach to producing and hearing electronic music – one that Benjamin might not have imagined.

Because music criticism is often wedded to ideas of the 'beautiful', it has always made writing about electronic music a parallel or 'other' to what is still referred to as 'classical music'. Although I have generally avoided the academic debates associated with aesthetics, this book leans into Edmund Burke's notion of the sublime as unfamiliar, astonishing and discontinuous, not surprisingly aligning it in the mid-twentieth century with the controversial, dissonant qualities of 'new music'. Theoretically, the work of Gilles Deleuze on repetition and networks has been indispensable in understanding how technologies like tape loops, feedback loops and generative systems continue to challenge musical thinking.

The protagonists of this book – musicians and engineers – have not generally worked from philosophical or aesthetic ideals, but instead have proceeded from more pragmatic, experimental and material premises. The outcomes of these collaborative efforts have, nonetheless, led to more nuanced and complex thinking about music, culture and society.

Electronic music is no longer elite. Arguably, most of the sonic signals of our daily lives are electronic. What began as the otherworldly sounds of Bebe and Louis Barron's film score for the 1956 film *Forbidden Planet*, and the rarefied, new timbres of Stockhausen's *Kontakte* a few years later, are now a common part of our soundscape. Even electro-sonic debris – glitches, bursts of amplitude and frequency modulated radio transmissions, fragments of media speech and noise – have found their way into our lives.

The rise of a new 'audio culture' has granted free admission to previously excluded technologies of sound production and listening, and has revolutionized musical thought.[2] Increasingly we are listening to electronic sounds, thinking about them, finding new meanings in them, experimenting with them and re-hearing them as listeners and makers. What is at stake here is huge, and I am guided by Jacques Attali's brilliant axiom that 'Music is more than an object of study: it is a way of perceiving the world.'[3]

The chapters in this book are organized around specific technologies that emerged in the twentieth century: the tape recorder, tube and transistor circuitry, the turntable and the phonograph recording, the microphone and the computer. These material objects were not simply invented and then put to use musically. Each of these technologies followed its own course, weaving between the logic and potentialities of engineering and musical thinking. Often, composers and musicians have imagined how electronic music might sound before the actual technology was in place to realize it. Edgard Varèse famously described electronic instruments in his lectures and writing well before they were actually developed. 'Possible music' sometimes preceded the actual appearance of the material instrument that could bring it into sensory existence. This is not to say that electronic music has always existed like a Platonic form. More often, the 'thing' itself was designed with one purpose in mind, only to be rediscovered in the real time of musical practice as a very different entity.

In general terms, there is always an important distinction to be made between the design and original purpose of a technology and its cultural application. Often, the very word 'technology' is associated with modernity, but it is worth recalling that technologies have existed throughout human history, expanding the reach of the body and mind. The shovel is a technology. The book is a technology, a perfect one, I'd say. Most technologies reach their point of perfection at some stage. The violin reached its perfection in Italy in the early eighteenth century. The Hammond organ reached its pinnacle in 1954 with the model B-3. The tube amplifier, a technology that is over one hundred years old, is still considered the *sine qua non* of a rock guitarist's sound. The original discrete-circuit, transformer-balanced Trident and Neve recording consoles of the 1970s are still considered the best sounding, and command astronomical prices.

However, few technologies are static in their use. The violin and piano, for example, have been played more or less conventionally for centuries, although electronic technology has afforded them a new musical life through amplification and other kinds of processing. All electronic musicians understand that analogue technology is alive and well. The most highly capitalized studios in the world will often have a two-inch, 24-track analogue tape recorder available as a tracking tool, since many musicians still hear the analogue recording as superior to the digital recording. This unsettled relationship of analogue and digital technology is one of the most exciting and challenging aspects of the ongoing history of electronic music.

Although this book is organized around specific technologies, it privileges the moments of creative disruption when the mind and hand invent and reinvent cultural artefacts. I have tried to include direct accounts of composers, engineers and musicians as often as possible to bring these sonic inventions and human encounters to life. I have drawn upon memoirs, interviews, liner notes and personal communications to suggest the vast network of interactions that comprise the cultural history of this field. The following chapters are filled with anecdotes and reflections on musical practices and processes with an emphasis on how electronic music has transformed musical thought and vice versa. The innovators who shaped the technology and music range widely from isolated experimenters to classical musicians, jazz musicians, rock musicians, sound artists, recording engineers and the newer generations of electronic musicians doing hip-hop, house, techno, ambient and electronica. Some advances are epiphanies, some happy accidents, many others the result of years of experimentation and dedication.

Although discontinuities and interruptions figure importantly in this account of electronic music, I follow a fairly standard chronology in describing how musical thought and compositional practice has intersected with music technology from around 1945. There are some interesting earlier examples of course, but I locate its beginnings with Pierre Schaeffer's work in 1948 and the recorded sound pieces that he called *musique concrète*. Subsequently, Herbert Eimert's studio at the WDR radio station in Cologne, Vladimir Ussachevsky and Otto Luening's formation of a studio at Columbia University in New York, and Princeton composer Milton Babbitt's work with the RCA synthesizer marked the next stage, creating highly structured music by primarily electronic means. This body of work became known as 'classical electronic music'. At the same time, American composers on the West Coast such as Pauline Oliveros and Morton Subotnick began to refer to their work as 'tape music', which tended to be more freewheeling and improvisational. I tend to use the term 'electronic music' to refer generally to all of the electronic genres we encounter today, regardless of their sources, materials and techniques.

The sonic materials of electronic music are, and have always been, vast and generally uncodifiable. Composer Barney Child's outline of the aesthetics of indeterminacy have always seemed useful to me when thinking about approaching electronic music, because the composer's search for, generation of and organization of electronic sounds has often involved the use of techniques of indeterminacy, found sound, improvisation, unorthodox signal flow and unorthodox electronic settings. Taking the aesthetic assumptions of indeterminacy to a logical end,

> Any sound or no sound at all is as valid, as 'good' as any other sound . . . each sound is a separate event . . . It need carry no implication of what has preceded it or will follow it . . . Any assemblage of sounds is as valid as any other . . . Any means of generating an assemblage of sounds is as valid as any other.[4]

This is not to say that any musical composition is as good as any other, but rather to recognize the boundless potentiality of electronic sound.

The search for new sounds has led composers to create their own electronic music instruments. It has been said, for instance, that Karlheinz Stockhausen was the first dub mixer because he wanted to do live mixing of his electronic pieces in the concert hall and asked his technicians at the WDR to design and build a compact mixer/controller. In another musical domain, King Crimson guitarist Robert Fripp invented what is now the rock guitarist's ubiquitous pedalboard, a collection of various individual effects (or 'stompboxes') mounted together and interconnected by short patch cords. The pedalboard has become the primary design space for the present-day guitarist's sound.

Often, an electronic technology has directly influenced musical performance practice, both playing techniques and the actual *sound* of the music. Elvis Presley's guitarist Scotty Moore purchased a Ray Butts EchoSonic – a guitar amplifier with a built-in tape delay system – because the band's live performances sounded so 'empty' to him. Sun Records producer Sam Phillips had been adding 'slapback' tape echo to many of Presley's recordings during this time and it had become a characteristic part of the band's recorded sound.[5] In effect, it was a technical connection of hardware that required Moore to imagine a new rhythmic relationship to Presley's music and actualize it by a combination of live playing and tape delay.

Music technology facilitated the practice of 'studio composition'. This is most apparent in rock music, beginning in the late 1960s and continuing to the present-day 'bedroom composer'. Rather than use the recording studio in its traditionally neutral role, Frank Zappa *composed* in the studio, using overdubs, tape splices and other effects to create collages of improvisation, impromptu weird conversations, atonal musical fragments and eccentric rock songs.

Brian Eno, when working with Talking Heads on the album *Fear of Music* or with David Bowie on his album *Low*, creatively staked out a liminal area between the roles of composer and producer. Like Zappa, the studio for him was a compositional sketchpad. Eno, who has often said with undue modesty that he is not really a musician, listed 'electronic treatments' as a creative credit for himself on *Fear of Music*. The idea was clear: Eno saw his role of electronically generating and processing musical material as a compositional act. Serendipitously, when I happened to come into possession of an EMS VCS-3 analogue synthesizer – the very kind that Eno himself used – I found that the signal processing section of the patchbay (ring modulation, reverberation and so on) was labelled 'treatments'. This, for me, was a striking example of the crosstalk between technology and musical practice that animates this book.

It would be hard to overemphasize the material and cultural importance of the analogue synthesizer, developed in the 1960s, in expanding and defining what and especially *how* musicians and composers made their music. Its portability allowed composers and musicians to begin to do live performances, and its relatively lower cost also meant that electronic music was no longer relegated to established studios. As the tape recorder itself became more available to musicians, electronic music and 'tape composition' began to flourish in pop, rock and jazz.

Similarly, the advent of the digital synthesizer, drum machine, digital recorder, effects processors and guitar pedals completely transformed popular music. DIY culture has given us circuit bending, the practice of tearing apart and rewiring electronic toys and devices as sound-making devices. These days composers and musicians are almost as likely to arrive at a gig with a laptop as a traditional musical instrument.

So, there exist these various technologies of electronic music, old and new, a continuum from which musicians and composers cycle, recycle and remix. What is missing from this description and what completes this musical circuitry is, of course, the listener. The varieties of electronic music require and have, in fact, developed in tandem with new ways of hearing music. It is not simply that younger or more practised listeners are uniquely suited to experimentation through their openness and experience with new media, but that electronic music, insomuch as it is a cultural as well as a technical apparatus, is situated differently from how earlier music was in its time. As musicologist Zofia Lissa points out, many important musical shifts in Western music (for instance, the transition from Gregorian chant to early tenth-century polyphony) have been accompanied by concurrent shifts in listening practices. In terms of listening 'backwards', historically speaking, Lissa invokes the example of Western monophonic music – Gregorian chant to the beginnings of polyphony about AD 900 – to point out that

> Monodic music sounds differently today from what it must have sounded in the ear of the listener who saw the nascence of monody and subsequently was familiar with the various phases in its development. Listening to monodic music today, we are unable to extricate ourselves from what to us sounds like its harmonic content; we infuse melodic structures with a harmonic content which emerges from our own musical thinking.[6]

How this is the case has been an issue of extended debate beyond the scope of this book. However, the obvious attachment to ear buds and headphones suggests a kind of cybernetic model that has altered the acoustical space of listening. Again, this 'different ear', enhanced by an electronic prosthesis, feeds back into the psycho-acoustic spaces of our lives – thus we hear everything differently. In trying to understand this shift, Ola Stockfelt's theory of 'adequate modes of listening' is ultimately the most inclusive and democratic. Stockfelt sees the current musical landscape as one in which

> Each hearing person who listens to the radio, watches TV, goes to the movies, goes dancing . . . has built up, has been *forced* (in order to be able to handle her or his perceptions of the sound) – to build up an appreciable competence in translating and using the music impressions that stream in from loudspeakers in almost every living space . . . Thus, to listen adequately hence does not mean any particular, better, or 'more musical,' 'more intellectual,' or 'culturally superior' way of listening. It means that one masters and develops the ability to listen for what is relevant to the genre in the music.[7]

Finally, a book about technology is necessarily technical. Technical terminology and sometimes close descriptions of the electronic and psycho-acoustic processes are essential. Ultimately, it is all in the details. As a composer, and the son of an aeronautical engineer, I have been repeatedly convinced that small imprecisions in parts can bring down the whole plane or project. While I have tried to be meticulous in describing technological developments, it is the interplay among composers, performers and machines that motivates my writing and powers the trajectory of this book. Electronic music – understood as a material, social and artistic dynamic – has not only changed the modes of musical production but has, in its wide-ranging effects, transformed the very terms of musical thought.

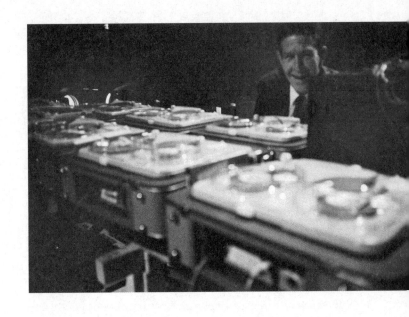

John Cage with tape recorders, Hamburg, 1966.

1
TAPE RECORDER

The reproduction of sound inaugurated one of the most significant cultural shifts of the last century. What happened is clear: the continuous flow of sounds all around us could be captured and allowed to spin free from their sources. This disconnection of sound from source required new conceptualizations of sound production and sound reception. To begin to understand the huge cognitive, philosophical and psychological impact of the emergence of this new 'audio culture',[1] let us search out one thing that propelled this massive change. What singular material apparatus so completely changed our aural existence? There can be only one answer: the tape recorder.

The history of the visual arts offers some analogies for beginning with the tape recorder. In his book *The Reconfigured Eye: Visual Truth in the Post-photographic Era*, William J. Mitchell relates two events that are crucial in the history of visual representation. Pliny tells of a Corinthian maiden who traces the shadow of her lover and so invents drawing and painting. William Henry Fox Talbot traces an image at Lake Como using a camera obscura, and then turns his attention towards chemically fixing a shadow on treated paper. Along with the French daguerreotype, photography is born. Mitchell defines the photographic image as 'an analog representation of space in a scene'.[2]

Extending Mitchell's definition of the photographic image and taking into account the fact that sound is a time-based event, one can understand sound recording as an analogue representation of a sound or a sequence of sounds in an acoustic space or 'scene'. The tape recorder, as it developed, established the conditions for the creation of new sounds and new musics, including what came to be called 'electronic music'. And, just as the photograph ignited debates around the status of art and reality, so, too, the tape recorder began a seemingly never-ending questioning of the status of sound as 'music'.

Restart: The Modern Tape Recorder, A Brief History

In 1934 I. G. Farben (BASF), in cooperation with AEG, produced about 150,000 ft (45 km) of the first modern recording tape – oxide attached to a plastic backing. This quickly propelled the development of AEG's Magnetophon K1. They unveiled their recorder and flexible coated tape the next year at the Berlin Radio Fair, one of the most important industrial exhibitions in Europe. They also hosted a concert at their Feierabendhaus in Ludwigshafen am Rhein, with Sir Thomas Beecham conducting Mozart's Symphony No. 39 with the London Philharmonic Orchestra. The entire concert was recorded on magnetic tape.[3]

The Magnetophon was first used at the Reichs-Rundfunk Gesellschaft (RRG) in 1938. It was adopted on an experimental basis because the machine was still undergoing a great deal of development. Its signal-to-noise ratio was low and distortion was still a problem, and it was therefore unacceptable for professional use. It was not until 1940 that a researcher at the RRG, Walter Weber, accidentally discovered what became known as 'high-frequency biasing', through which the Magnetophon could offer the frequency response and lower distortion that tape recording promised.[4] As a medium, magnetic tape offered better fidelity, ten times the length of a wax disc recording, immediate playback, reuse of the tape for future recordings and significant ease of editing.

At the close of the Second World War, a u.s. Army Signal Corps officer had the opportunity to hear one of the advanced Magnetophons in use at the RRG in Berlin:

> The technician placed a roll of tape on one of the machines and started it. Suddenly, out of complete silence, an orchestra bloomed into being with fidelity such as I have never heard in my life. From deep resonant bass to the shimmering of the flute it was all there. It was clean! It was free from any noticeable distortion. And if that were not enough, the dynamic range was fantastic compared with anything I had ever experienced.[5]

Returning to San Francisco with the Magnetophon schematics and specs, the officer, Jack Mullin, worked with a partner in the film business to build a prototype version of the German machine with American electronics. A small electronics company in California, Ampex would be the first American firm to build commercial tape recorders based on Mullin's design. The Ampex 200A immediately garnered the interest and approval of singer Bing Crosby and ABC Radio. The rest of the entertainment industry got on board very quickly.

By the end of the 1940s, many u.s. companies had begun to compete in the market for professional-level tape recorders, but also in the growing world of 'audiophiles'. This term was apparently coined in 1951 by *High Fidelity* magazine to describe very serious music listeners, usually record collectors, who insisted on having sophisticated audio equipment in their homes.

The first commercial tape recorders became available in the 1950s, but were not widely purchased by the general public. The high cost of recording tape relegated the tape recorder to the small circle of audiophiles. Even the introduction of stereophonic recording in the mid-1950s failed to do much for the tape recorder. With the advent of transistor technology, the smaller, lighter quarter-track home tape recorders of the late 1960s and '70s fared better, but it was not until the introduction of the 'cassette tape' in the early 1970s that the consumer market took up tape recording fully.

In the meantime, the heavy commercial tape recorders made by Ampex, and later Scully, became the primary tool of the U.S. radio and record industry, and tape music composers. Professional modern recording tape, usually a quarter-inch or half-inch in width, is easy to edit. The higher tape speed (15 and 30 inches per second) of the professional machines produce extremely high-fidelity recordings. As the medium developed in the recording industry, recording sessions and editing sessions began to become separate events in the recording process. This latter development is highly significant in the history of music. It was precisely when tape became easily editable that the creative possibilities of the tape recorder began to manifest themselves.

Musique concrète

Musique concrète, originating in France in the late 1940s, can be considered the first truly modern electronic music. To put this radical musical departure in brief context, it is important to recall that contemporary music in postwar Paris was synonymous with Nadia Boulanger and her elite circle of composers. With little or no contact with the Parisian musical scene, Pierre Schaeffer, a sound engineer at Radiodiffusion Française (now Radiodiffusion-Télévision Française, or RTF), was inspired in 1948 to create a concert using new sound materials, which he called *Concert de bruits* (Concert of Noises), to be broadcast on the radio. Preemptively, the question of whether the sounds produced in the radio broadcast and in subsequent collaborations with Pierre Henry and others were truly 'music' was posed by their creator, Schaeffer himself. In a gesture that perhaps was meant to ward off the inevitable scandal and misapprehension that he and his cohort were out to destroy Western music, he insisted in a programme note that they merely intended to 'add to it' through a new use of recording, 'an art of sound': 'traditional music is not denied: anymore than the theater is supplanted by the cinema. Something new is added, a new art of sound. Am I wrong in still calling it music?'[6]

Although this question of artistic legitimacy continued throughout his career, Schaeffer's process of making a 'new art of sound' was unique. With the idea for his *Concert de bruits* in mind, Schaeffer had begun earlier that year to collect various mundane sound-making objects such as doorbells, alarm clocks, bells, rattles and children's toys, later adding resonators from a pipe organ destroyed in the war. Experimenting with these materials in his Studio d'Essai, he was initially frustrated. The sounds immediately seemed too referential to him ('glass', 'bell', 'wood', 'metal'). Unsure of himself, Schaeffer continued with experiments that produced two epiphanies. The first was the creation of a combined attack of noise and pitch (a melodic element added to a percussive element) from his home-made 'instruments'. The second he discovered after entering the studio to record the instruments, with each sound cut on a separate disc with his record lathe. (It is important to note that Schaeffer worked with recorded discs at that time. Tape recorders did not appear at RTF until about 1951.) During this recording process, Schaeffer hit upon the idea to remove the beginning (attack) of the bell sounds, leaving only the remaining parts – the steady-state and decay: 'Without its percussion [attack transients], the bell becomes an oboe sound. I prick up my ears. Has a breach appeared in the enemy ranks? Has the advantage changed sides?'[7]

Schaeffer also imagined what would one day become known as a sampler, an instrument with an 'organ' keyboard with each key linked to a turntable. Each turntable would have a library of discs (one sound per disc) that could contain 'every conceivable instrument, musical or not'.[8] He realized that his idea, while possible, was not technically practical at that time. He returned to his experiments but composed nothing.

Two months later, a still frustrated Schaeffer, 'looking for a shortcut', entered the Batignolles station in Paris with a mobile sound crew from RTF, intending to create a 'concert of railway engines'. By chance, there were six engines in the station. The drivers were willing to 'improvise' with their engines. Each had a remarkably different sonic character. He returned to his RTF studio to cut discs of the recordings. By dropping and picking up the needle, he was able to isolate rhythmic segments of the trains, and by altering the speed of the turntables was able to transform some of the railway sounds in such a way that they become new sounds. When completed, the more modestly titled *Étude aux chemins de fer* (Railway Study) marked the beginning of a new music with a new name:

I have coined the term *Musique Concrète* for this commitment to compose with materials taken from a 'given' experimental sound in order to emphasize our dependence, no longer on preconceived sound abstractions, but on sound fragments that exist in reality and that are considered as discrete and complete sound objects, even if and above all when they do not fit in with the elementary definitions of music theory.[9]

Schaeffer's careful steps in formulating *musique concrète* had much to do with his changing modes of hearing recorded sounds. He referred to these perceptual differences as 'dramatic' (referential) and musical (pure sound), deciding that hearing the train sounds as a 'dramatic sequence' constrained the listener's imagination. As he proceeded, he discovered that simple repetitions of a sound event could go a long way towards causing the referent of a sound to float freely from the sound matter itself. Schaeffer also realized that the listener has agency in regard to hearing the sound for itself, its timbre, texture, internal rhythm and so on.

Schaeffer eventually included the *Railway Study* in his 1948 *Quatre Études de bruits* (Four Noise Studies). Listening to the *Railway Study*, one is aware immediately of an underlying pulse to the music. As the piece unfolds, syncopations and polyrhythms created by the intercut segments decontextualize the train sounds enough to provide at least a glimpse into Schaeffer's developing ideas around acousmatics.

Several of these pieces are particularly significant but creative failures. The *Étude aux tourniquets* (Whirligig Study) utilizes a child's toy that spins or whirls, a xylophone, bells and three zanzis as its sound sources. The opening percussive sounds of the piece are much less referential than the *Railway Study*, using lockout-groove loops to create a rhythmic structure. The pitched elements that follow recall more traditionally 'musical' string and xylophone events. In fact, Schaeffer had tried to record segments of music scored by a friend. This proved to be a failure, and Schaeffer then decided to use short segments during the odd moments of the recording session. Given the nature of the source material, these pitched

sound fragments are quite innocent and childlike. At the end of
the composition, these loops are finally dispersed into the ether
by the use of a fadeout of heavy reverberation.

Étude pathétique (Study on Pots and Pans) begins with the
sounds of spinning lids of pots and pans. These are followed by
various looped and layered vocal and musical sounds including
a canal barge, a harmonica and a recording of French actor
Sacha Guitry. Schaeffer's use of looped coughs and popular song
fragments makes this the most playful – even provocative – piece
of the études. The return of the pots and pans does little formally
to dispel the humorous moments preceding it. I say provocative,
because this étude has a sense of humour that works precisely
because of its references to the human.

The *Étude violette* has a reflective, dreamlike quality. It
opens with heavily reverberated piano fragments played by the
composer Pierre Boulez. Schaeffer had given Boulez the task of
playing different styles of Classical, Romantic and Impressionistic
music. Reversed piano chords and slow-speed events are layered
with percussive events. Occasional loops enter and then recede.
Three electronic beeps signal the end of the piece.

On 5 October 1948 Schaeffer broadcast the études on
radio, calling them a *Concert of Noises*. Public reaction was
mixed. Listeners were variously intrigued and insulted. In
1949 the composer Pierre Henry joined Schaeffer in the RTF
studio. Trained as a composer and percussionist at the Paris
Conservatoire, Henry quickly took a leading role, becoming a
'turntable genius' according to Schaeffer, creating hundreds
of sound objects, samples and sequences with Schaeffer's
variable-speed disc-cutting invention. Their 1950 collaboration,
Symphonie pour un homme seul (Symphony for a Lone Man), is a
substantial twelve-movement work that uses sounds only of the
human body:

The lone man had to find his symphony within himself, not by simply thinking up music in the abstract but by being his own instrument. A lone man possesses much more than the twelve notes of the trained voice. He shouts, he whistles, he punches, he laughs, he groans. His heart beats, his breathing accelerates, he pronounces words, calls out, and others call in reply. Nothing echoes a lone cry more than the hubbub of the crowd.[10]

To connect the entire human body – including but not limited to the voice – to his new electronic medium was inspired.

It seems fair to say in retrospect that Schaeffer is a brilliant musical thinker, but not an accomplished composer. On the other hand, Henry's contributions to the composition of *Symphony for a Lone Man* and to the project of *musique concrète* in general are musically profound. Together, they consolidated a new art form – with Schaeffer as a 'producer', in the present-day sense, and Henry as a composer – that would legitimize the music in the eyes of a sceptical press and begin to create serious interest from classical avant-garde composers from around the world.

In 1951 their partnership, the Groupe de Recherches de Musique Concrète (GRMC), established a purpose-built electroacoustic music studio at RTF. It was at this time that the first commercial magnetic tape recorders arrived at RTF. The first composition workshop on *musique concrète* took place at the GRMC that same year. Present were composers Pierre Boulez, Jean Barraque and Michel Philippot, who later became Schaeffer's assistant.

Over the next two years, preeminent modernist composers Olivier Messiaen and Karlheinz Stockhausen, and Boulez, created *musique concrète* pieces at the experimental studio. Boulez composed *Étude I* and *Étude II* in 1951, followed by

Messiaen's *Timbres-durées* and Stockhausen's *Konkrete Etüde* in 1952. In 1954 Edgard Varèse worked there on the tape parts of his *Déserts*. The Greek architect and composer Iannis Xenakis joined the GRMC that same year.

Despite the historical confluence of technological innovation and creativity at the GRMC, there were false starts and brilliant concepts that exceeded the limits of the technology of the time. A composer whose sonic imagination was far ahead of the technological curve, for instance, Edgard Varèse composed only one tape-alone composition in his small musical output, largely owing to his frustrations with the lack of technology available to him at the time. Although he imagined the powerful possibilities of an electronic music, it would be several decades before the technology existed that would allow this possible music to be realized. In 1936 Varèse described his creative dilemma:

> When new instruments allow me to write music as I conceive it, the movement of sound-masses, of shifting planes will clearly be perceived in my work, taking the place of linear counterpoint. When these sound masses collide, the phenomenon of penetration or repulsion will seem to occur. Certain transmutations taking place on certain planes will seem to be projected onto other planes, moving at different speeds and angles . . . The entire work will flow as a river flows.[11]

Poème électronique, produced in 1958 at the Philips studio in Paris, is a composition that has fascinated and inspired many composers since its premiere. Primarily an example of *musique concrète*, the piece contains some abstract sounds, produced with oscillators and filters. Installed at Le Corbusier's Philips Pavilion at the 1958 World's Fair in Brussels, the piece was spatialized, moving around the structure via 350 loudspeakers.

Other early experimental pieces remained only suggestive of the musical future but this singular work by Varèse is rightly recognized by both electronic and non-electronic musicians as a masterwork.

Another exceptional figure in this history, Iannis Xenakis, also prefigured current practices such as algorithmic composition and new sound synthesis techniques. His 1958 composition *Concret P-H* is an example of a whole new concept of tape splicing using a recording of smouldering charcoal as the sole sound source. In the liner notes of the original recording, Xenakis described how he challenged the usual way of manipulating concrete sound by taking a single sound event and then atomizing it:

> Start with a sound made up of many particles, then see how you can make it change imperceptibly, growing and develop-ing, until an entirely new sound results . . . This was in defiance of the usual manner of working with concrète sounds. Most of the musique concrète which had been produced up to the time of *Concret P-H* is full of many abrupt changes and juxtaposed sections without transitions. This happened because the original recorded sounds used by the composers consisted of a block of one kind of sound, then a block of another, and did not extend beyond this.[12]

This technique is suggestive of the 'granulation' techniques used in present-day sound synthesis. The piece was installed at the Philips Pavilion along with *Poème électronique*. It seems somehow fitting that these two visionary composers' works would be presented together so early in the nascent history of electronic music.

Pierre Henry directed the GRMC from 1952 until 1958, when his differences with Schaeffer caused his resignation. Henry went on to compose some of the first major works of *musique concrète*. The breadth and sophistication of his technique is evident in *Le Microphone bien tempéré* (The Well-tempered Microphone, 1950–52), the ten sections of which range from Surrealist effects to more systematic treatments. Henry began collaborating with choreographer Maurice Béjart in 1954, producing *Haut-voltage* (High Voltage, 1956), *Le Voyage* (The Voyage, 1962), *La Reine verte* (The Green Queen, 1963), and *Variations pour une porte et un soupir* (Variations on a Door and a Sigh, 1963).

Luc Ferrari's Inadvertent Masterpiece

Composer Luc Ferrari became a member of the GRMC in 1958, and on its dissolution that year reformed it with Schaeffer as the Groupe de Récherche Musicale. Arguably the most important piece produced at the GRM, Luc Ferrari's *Presque rien No. 1: Le Lever du jour au bord de la mer* (Almost Nothing: Dawn at the Seaside, 1970) has mythic status in present-day electroacoustic music circles. It currently stands as a foundational musical composition due, in large part, to its historical position in the expanded frame of what is now called sound art, its provocative stance vis à vis *musique concrète*, and its radical understatedness.

The composer provided a concise history of the piece in a 1998 interview:

> I wanted to be as radical as possible, and take it to the limit in terms of using natural sound, by not including any artificial, sophisticated sound at all . . . There's one landscape, a given time, and the radical thing is precisely that it's just one place at one specific time, daybreak. What's nice about the 'Presque Rien' is that you really notice the things you hear, and eventually there's a moment where sounds stand out more than they

normally would. I went everywhere with my tape recorder and microphone, and I was in this Dalmatian fishing village, and our bedroom window looked out on a tiny harbour of fishing boats, in an inlet in the hills, almost surrounded by hills – which gave it an extraordinary acoustic. It was very quiet . . . I heard this silence which, little by little, began to be embellished . . . It was amazing. I started recording at night, always at the same time when I woke up, about 3 or 4 a.m., and I recorded until about 6 a.m. I had a lot of tapes! And then I hit upon an idea – I recorded those sounds which repeated every day: the first fisherman passing by same time every day with his bicycle, the first hen, the first donkey, and then the lorry which left at 6 a.m. to the port to pick up people arriving on the boat. Events determined by society.[13]

Ferrari's piece was released on the prestigious Deutsche Gramophone's Avant-garde series in 1972. Inclusion in this elite series that featured the most highly regarded figures in postwar European new music did not, however, translate into respect from his musical peers. At its premiere, Ferrari recalls that the piece was 'badly received by my GRM colleagues, who said it wasn't music!'[14]

More 'unheard' than misunderstood, the piece was marginalized for years within a musical historiography that rendered it scarcely audible or, in effect, *inaudible* without the technical/theoretical listening apparati that could contribute to and fulfil its meaning. It came into its full aesthetic and auditory meaning twenty years later, when the expectations of listeners had moved past earlier debates and assumptions about the limits of music.

The language of early reviewers is instructive in this regard. For instance, an article appearing in a 1972 issue of the British contemporary music journal *Tempo* described *Presque rien* as a 'charmingly inactive chunk of *musique vérité*'.[15] This language of passivity and referentiality reminds us of the ways that new music could be equated with rigour, abstraction and most of all non-referentiality. This piece is clearly referential but it would be mistaken to see this as naive or easy.

Furthermore, the title of the review, 'Stockhausen and Others', reflects the background into which Ferrari's offering recedes. In a critical differentiation, the author establishes Stockhausen as the avant-garde's 'problem-solver *par excellence*'. The gist of the review is that the Ferrari disc, along with several others reviewed in the same article, is unworthy of our attention, compared to the masterpieces of Boulez, Berio and Stockhausen and, of course, that the task of the true artist/ composer was to struggle with a series of largely theoretical problems. In postwar Europe, this ideology of progress and the new was dominant. Of course, this ideology has remained in some circles the established trope of contemporary musical thought. Without diminishing the accomplishment of brilliant composers like Stockhausen, Boulez or Berio or even diminishing their importance in the narrower history of electronic music, it must be said that Ferrari's piece was far from naive or easy. To the contrary, with the advantage of retrospect, it opened windows onto possible musics that could only be fully engaged later in a very different place and a very different context.

Strikingly, the language of weakness and innocence (as opposed to the strength and rigour of the aforementioned composers) in the above review inadvertently reveals a future for the piece: 'The pity of it is that an innocent listener . . . would be perfectly justified in assuming that the majority of contemporary music was in an enfeebled state.'[16] Ironically, *Presque rien* ultimately revived a kind of innocence for the listener willing to be returned to the sonic world around her/him. This composition and Ferrari's own recollection of the piece as anecdotal in a temporal sense suggests a fresh interactive role for the listener:

> One day I went away . . . with a borrowed tape recorder. I did not travel very far, but nevertheless travelled a lot and I recorded things of life . . . music of a genre I called 'anecdotal music.' This means, I intended to produce a language that situates itself between the musical and the dramatic field. The employment of elements of reality allows me to tell a history, or allow the listener to create images, since the montages propose ambiguities.[17]

In retrospect, his respect for the active listener (rather than the concert audience) and his acknowledgement of a loose analogical frame for listening is quite radical. Theoretically, Ferrari's notion of 'anecdotal music' reopened the gates to the notion of analogy. Simply put, traditional classical music was ideally an abstraction. As he considered the limits of both *musique concrète* and *elektronische Musik*, Ferrari took the not inconsiderable risk of challenging the embargo on the use of directly recorded sound and its referential implications in electroacoustic composition. Instead of self-consciously abstracting the source material of *Presque rien*, this recorded 'reality' becomes a prompt for listeners to make sonic connections to their own conscious and unconscious processes. Constellations of sound analogies allow relationships – both similarities and differences – to emerge with the listener, rather than being directed by the composer. The audio recording might even be said to surpass the mimetic power of photography and visual realism because it is a time-based medium.

Tape Music Composition

Schaeffer's ideas remained musically interesting and provocative, especially within the confines of European new music. However, composers – particularly in the u.s. – began to develop their own ways of working the new music medium, increasingly referring to their music as 'Tape Music Composition'. No longer relying solely on Schaeffer's aesthetic assumptions, American composers took the new medium even further.

One of the more interesting early interventions in tape composition was, not surprisingly, John Cage's *Imaginary Landscape No. 5*, written in 1952. The score for this composition is a tape recorder tabulature (a form of musical notation indicating fingering rather than the pitch of notes). The content is supplied by the 'performer' who chooses any 42 long-playing records. The score is in graph form, where each unit equals 3 inches of recording tape. At a tape speed of 15½ inches per second, each unit then lasts one-fifth of a second. Cage's score also specifies the relative dynamics of each tape splice on a scale of one to eight. One number specified a constant amplitude, two numbers a crescendo or decrescendo, and three numbers 'more espressivo',[18] and where each recorded sound is to change, the actual sound being chosen from the 42 records previously decided upon. The radical idea here was that the sonic content is variable for each realization of the piece, but the tape lengths spliced together to make the music – effectively metrical proportions – mean that the formal structure is always fixed.

San Francisco Tape Music Center

In 1961 Ramon Sender and a group of composers around Robert Erickson's class at the San Francisco Conservatory put together a tape music studio. Sender's experiments doing 'sound on sound' with the school's Ampex tape recorder led him to the conclusion that contemporary composers must embrace the compositional possibilities of the medium. In 1962 the group moved to a new location that Sender and composer Morton Subotnick had found to become the San Francisco Tape Music Center. Their equipment was modest, including sine- and square-wave generators on loan from the Conservatory. Other experimental composers working there included Terry Riley, Steve Reich, Joseph Byrd and Robert Ashley. The San Francisco composers had no stake in the coming rift between *musique concrète* and *elektronische Musik* in Europe, preferring a less theoretically charged aesthetic.

The San Francisco Tape Music Center was in many ways unique. Whereas most studios around the world were institutionally sponsored, it was conceived of as a non-academic, public-access space for composers. The studio also fostered performances and collaborations that included artists involved in improvisation, mixed media, experimental theatre and happenings with innovative figures such as Bruce Baillie and Stan Brakhage.

New York: Columbia-Princeton Electronic Music Center

What would eventually become the Columbia-Princeton Electronic Music Center first resided in composer Vladimir Ussachevsky's living room. In 1955 he and his colleague Otto Luening were given space to create a studio. The new studio, housed in part of the former Bloomingdale Insane Asylum, fostered the burgeoning work of the two composers.[19] In 1959, with a grant from the Rockefeller Foundation, Ussachevsky and Luening, along with Princeton composers Milton Babbitt and Roger Sessions, established the Columbia-Princeton Electronic Music Center at Columbia University in New York City. Over the next twenty years, many composers worked there, including Bülent Arel, Luciano Berio, Mario Davidovsky, Daria Semegen, Pril Smiley, Alice Shields, Charles Wuorinen, Wendy Carlos and Edgard Varèse. Where the San Francisco Tape Music Center produced much more experimental, free-wheeling tape music, the Columbia-Princeton Center quickly became associated with the ideas of European classical electronic music and, eventually, computer-generated sound.

Schaeffer's Technological Legacy

The initial development of the tape recorder was as a purely recording device, through which sound could simply be captured and stored. However, the tape recorder quickly began to take on dual roles. The first was as a recording device, but as composers began to see its possibilities, the tape recorder became the primary compositional device in tape composition studios. Schaeffer's early studio techniques using turntables provided him the possibilities of speed manipulation, reverse direction and lock-out groove loops. The new medium of magnetic tape allowed composers to use, in addition to speed and direction changes, tape splicing techniques. This capability effectively made a reel of recording tape a random-access storage device. Much in the way film editing works, the tape composer could reorder, delete and even copy the material stored on tape. The tape recorder also provided the composer with the possibilities of creating tape loops and tape echo effects.

Just as Edgard Varèse had imagined the electronic music medium long before it existed, Schaeffer's sonic-mechanical developments adumbrate the whole history of electroacoustic music. It seems that the whole future of electronic music history is presaged here!

Schaeffer's earlier instrumental imaginings finally became possible with the arrival of the first magnetic tape recorders at RTF. The chromatic sound machine he had imagined earlier was designed and built by the Tolana Company in 1953. The chromatic Phonogène had a one-octave keyboard coupled to a twelve-capstan tape path loaded with a single loop of tape. When a key was depressed on the small keyboard, it would bring one of the twelve capstans and pinch-rollers into operation. The different-sized capstans caused the machine's single tape loop to be played from low speed to high speed, effectively transposing the pitch up and down in equal-tempered half-steps.[20] There was also a transposing switch on the keyboard, so the effective range was two octaves. Schaeffer's invention laid the conceptual and technical foundations for tape-loop instruments like the Mellotron and, eventually, one of the most important and widespread compositional practices of present-day electronic music: digital sampling.

About ten years later, a commercially minded inventor named Harry Chamberlin had been developing a keyboard instrument in California that also used tape-loop playback. Chamberlin's idea was not to use his invention to find new sounds, but rather to play a range of carefully recorded string, brass, wind, voice and keyboard notes on his keyboard.[21] In 1962 the company's salesman absconded with two of Chamberlin's Model 600s to England, where he removed the labels and sold the devices to a company that began to manufacture and sell them as 'Mellotrons'. After the resulting legal dispute was settled, Mellotrons were then manufactured legally and began to infiltrate rock music recordings.

John Lennon was intrigued by the Mellotron and wanted to use it on the Beatles' 'Strawberry Fields Forever' session. George Martin, the Beatles' producer, intensely disliked the instrument: 'It was as if a Neanderthal piano had impregnated a primitive electronic keyboard.'[22] Fortunately, this time Martin's taste lost out. The song begins famously with Paul McCartney's iconic introduction, with the sound of the Mellotron's noisy string progression capturing a sense of memory, longing and innate psychedelia.

The Mellotron was used heavily on the Moody Blues' *Days of Future Passed* album, creating a sound, and a form – the concept album – that marked the beginnings of progressive rock. Shortly after, the Mellotron found its place as a defining sound of three leading progressive rock bands of the late 1960s: King Crimson, Genesis and Tangerine Dream. In their music, the Mellotron was never mistaken for a real orchestra, but instead began to find its place among a whole new range of expansive electroacoustic textures. The sonic integration of the Mellotron is particularly apparent in the recordings of Tangerine Dream's *Phaedra* and *Rubycon*.

Perhaps the most inventive Mellotron composition is Robert Wyatt's 'Immediate Curtain', the final track on Matching Mole's first album. A major departure from his work with Soft Machine, his group Matching Mole (a play on words: *machine molle* is French for Soft Machine) focused on what Wyatt called 'simple songs' rather than the longer, complex music of his previous group.[23] The sustained, moody, mostly Mellotron solo is an unexpectedly dark ending to the rest of the record – rambunctious free-jazz/fusion tracks interspersed with Wyatt's eccentric vocals. Quiet improvisation from the band quickly gives way to what Wyatt self-deprecatingly described as 'fiddling about on the Mellotron'.[24] It is a wonderful, intuitive piece of neo-tonal music that at its best moments brings to mind the music of Gustav Holst.

Other Phonogènes

Schaeffer developed two other Phonogènes in the early 1950s. The Sliding Phonogène offered a continuously variable playback speed with either a tape loop or standard tapes wound on reels. The Universal Phonogène was a variant that allowed the pitch and speed of the playback to be controlled separately.

In the era of magnetic tape, disentangling a taped sound's pitch and temporal duration was not a trivial problem. In the mid-1950s, a group of acoustic researchers came up with a novel tape-splicing technique to produce this effect manually. This involved recording the word 'Hello', the utterance lasting 0.5 seconds, at a tape speed of 7.5 inches per second. They continued by

> slowing down the original *hello* to half-speed, produced a one-octave drop, with the expected slow, 'fog horn,' sound characteristic of slowed-down tapes. This was now recorded onto a 7.5 i.p.s. tape, so that the sound section was 7.5 inches long. The sound section was cut into ten equal parts, each .075 in. in length, and these were sequentially numbered from one to ten. The even parts were discarded, and the odd parts were spliced in the order 1, 3, 5, 7, 9. This produced an *Hello* of the original duration but one octave lower.[25]

From this point, it was simply a matter of figuring out how to do this technique mechanically. The problem was solved by the use of a revolving disc in the tape path that was equipped with equally spaced multiple playback heads (usually two, four or six). The Springer Company in Germany produced a version of such a machine used by the composer Stockhausen in his 1967 composition *Hymnen*. This technique is effectively a mechanical means to granulate sound, a powerful technique used much later in digital sound synthesis.

Three-head Tape Recorder

Schaeffer's Three-head Tape Recorder was a 1952 invention that allowed for three different tapes to be played back in sync with each other, thus creating three-part polyphony. The idea of multiple, discrete recording tracks had also been an idea of the American guitarist Les Paul for many years, though his desire was much less abstract than Schaeffer's. Paul simply wanted to be able to play along and record a new track in sync with a pre-recorded track.

The design of the tape recorder contained both a problem and a promise. The sound material was recorded on one magnetic head, but played back on a separate head a few inches further down the tape path. Thus there was a time lag between the initially recorded sound and its reproduction through the amplifier and the speakers attached to it. Working with the Ampex Corporation in the mid-1950s, Paul helped develop an eight-track tape recorder with 'sel-sync' (selective synchronous recording), where monitoring off the recording head rather than the playback head allows musicians to play in sync with previously recorded tracks. Sel-sync recording constituted a radical change in the recording process. The ability to 'overdub', that is, play along live in sync with a pre-recorded track, meant that musicians had the capability to creatively re-insert themselves into the tape recorder's musical timeline.

Tape Delay

Schaeffer's Morphophone was a device that contained a tape loop spinning on the outside edge of a disc, with ten playback heads in contact with it. Each playback head also had its own pre-amplifier and filter arrangement. This invention was used primarily for reverberation and echo effects.[26] Here, the distance between the record and multiple playback heads was used to musical advantage. After recording a sound on the playback head, it would repeat each time it passed one of the ten playback heads. Depending on the tape speed, the resulting sound would be a series of echoes if the tape were moving relatively slowly, or a reverberated sound if the tape speed were sufficiently fast.[27]

From Censorship to the Echoplex

While Schaeffer imagined transforming sound by adding delay and echo processing, the commercial radio and music industry saw another use that took advantage of the fact that the tape recorder's record head and playback head were a few inches apart. The first broadcast profanity delay was invented in 1952 by an engineer at the radio station WKAP in Allentown, Pennsylvania. It consisted of a tape recorder with an external playback head spaced far enough away from the record head (between 3 and 6 ft, or 90 and 180 cm) to allow for a five-second delay. This system was introduced when WKAP started a talk show called *Open Mic*.

This was possible on any tape recorder. An engineer working for Vladimir Ussachevsky at Columbia, Peter Mauzey, had demonstrated this technique to him in about 1951.[28] By manually feeding the delayed output from the playback head back into the recording head, a series of echoes could be generated. Ussachevsky used this technique in his 1952 composition *Sonic Contours*, in which piano sounds are echoed and reverberated to create new rhythmic structures and dramatic dense sounds. That same year, his Columbia colleague Otto Luening composed

Low-speed, a piece that creates a series of ongoing, hypnotic rhythms by the use of tape echo.

The sound of tape echo is quite striking and musically compelling and has appealed to many different musicians in different genres. Eventually, commercially built tape-delay machines were produced. The Echoplex became available in 1959. It used a tape loop and incorporated a feedback control, the amplitude of the delayed signal, which would determine the number of iterations of the delayed sound. Eventually the Echoplex had a manually adjustable tape head that could alter the delay in real time.

Pianist Chick Corea modestly recounts the fabulous sounds he got with his electric piano and an Echoplex during his years with Miles Davis's band on recordings such as *Live at Fillmore* in 1970:

> There were a few pieces of effects gear that I would carry with me sometimes. One of them was a box called an 'Echoplex.' It was basically a little tape recorder that the signal passed through with an adjustable record head that enabled me to wiggle it while the sound was going through and get all manner of weird effects ... I also used an old ring modulator made, I think, by Oberheim.[29]

Composer Pauline Oliveros began working with tape-delay systems in the early 1960s. Her composition *Bye Bye Butterfly* is a live studio performance using two oscillators, a tape-delay system of two recorders, and a turntable playing a section of Puccini's *Madame Butterfly*. Oliveros improvised while the recording of Puccini played. The combination of the singer's voice and the swept oscillators is quite beautiful and disturbing. This kind of appropriation and revision was characteristic of some of the West Coast tape music composers such as Oliveros, Joseph Byrd and Frank Zappa. Oliveros's composition could be read as a critique of the treatment of women characters in the history of opera. This turn towards creativity as critique in the midst of the turbulent 1960s was apparent in much of the U.S. experimental music scene.

The Tape Loop

In the broadest sense, tape delay emulated the natural phenomena of echo and reverberation; the tape loop, on the other hand, is deliberately constructed as endless repetition. In fact, the sound of the tape loop is the most extreme example of 'surface repetition' in music. Even before composers began experimenting with tape recorders, the idea of an endlessly repeating musical structure occurred to Pierre Schaeffer, who used lock-out grooves to cause a deliberate skipped-record sound with his disc-cutting lathe. The tape recorder provided even more fertile ground, because a piece of tape could be cut out of the reel and each end spliced together to form a continuous, repeating sonic structure when played back.

The tape recorder itself must be jury-rigged in order to create a tape loop. First, a piece of tape is cut and spliced end-to-end. It must be threaded through the machine's tape path, past the playback head, and then around some heavy, moveable object. Composers often used a jar filled with marbles or a microphone stand. Tape loops can be of any length, so each configuration will present different physical requirements. The sound of the tape loop is sonically strange and uncanny because the same sounds arise but can be perceived as different over time.

Repetition is, of course, an important structural feature of all music. In most musical traditions around the world – indigenous, folk, classical and popular – one need not listen for very long until features of the music begin to manifest themselves by repetition. In the short term, we hear phrases repeated; in the longer term, whole sections frequently return, often verbatim. At many musical levels, repetition abounds, especially in popular music. In his essay on popular music, Theodor Adorno criticized its surface repetition, asserting that its standardization, its sameness, was stultifying and socially anaesthetizing:

> The frame of mind to which popular music originally appealed, on which it feeds, and which it perpetually reinforces, is simultaneously one of distraction and inattention. Listeners are distracted from the demands of reality by entertainment which does not demand attention either.[30]

Adorno describes one mode of listening to repetition that is distracted, passive and devoid of meaning. Repetition occurs differently to the attentive listener or composer who is attuned to musical memory.

A long philosophical tradition, beginning with St Augustine, argues for repetition as a necessary construction for creating meaning and memory over time:

> And I come to the fields and spacious palaces of my memory, where are the treasures of innumerable images, brought into it from things of all sorts perceived by the senses. There is stored up, whatsoever besides we think, either by enlarging or diminishing, or any other way varying those things which the sense hath come to; and whatever else hath been committed and laid up, which forgetfulness hath not yet swallowed up and buried ... These I drive away with the hand of my heart, from the face of my remembrance; until what I wish for be unveiled, and appear in sight, out of its secret place. Other things come up readily, in unbroken order, as they are called for; those in

front making way for the following; and as they make way, they are hidden from sight, ready to come when I will. All which takes place when I repeat a thing by heart.[31]

Samuel Butler's idea of repetition in his *Life and Habit* (1878) begins with the notion that in repetition we recognize what has come before by connecting the past to the present, and in doing so exhibit a deeper, unconscious form of knowledge.[32]

Likewise the contemporary philosopher Gilles Deleuze argues that in repetition, nothing is ever identical: that there is only difference. This is much in line with composers who find in the tape loop rich new levels of sonic detail, exciting motoric rhythms and even doorways to trance and ecstasy.

Steve Reich composed two pieces in 1965–6 using tape loops, *It's Gonna Rain* and *Come Out*. They differ insofar as they use two tape machines with the same material recorded on them, but rely on the subtly changing relationship of the two loops. While Reich's are important tape music compositions in their own right, the 'phasing' technique Reich began to develop richly fed his instrumental composition for years to come. He describes the making of *It's Gonna Rain*:

This is a process that I discovered by accident. I had two cheap tape [mono] recorders . . . I had a pair of stereo headphones with two separate plugs and I plugged one in the back of one machine and one into the back of the other, and made these two loops as identical as I could. I pushed the two start buttons and, by sheer chance, they started in unison. The odds are not too good for that to happen, but they did.

I had the stereo phones on and it felt like the sound was in the middle of my head. It seemed like it went from the left side of my head and down my arm and across the floor and then it began to reverberate. And finally, I got to this relationship that

– in my mind – was what I wanted to do, which was [sings] 'It's gonna, it's gonna, it's gonna, rain, rain.' It was the 180°, or the mid-point on top of each other. But what I realized was that it took several minutes to get to that position. This journey, this trip is far more interesting than that particular destination. There are all these irrational destinations in between.[33]

What Reich calls 'irrational destinations' would seem to refer to the fascinating phonemic phasing of his tape technique, where the parts of the utterance get shifted, reordered, syncopated and re-accented.

Jimi Hendrix took a different turn with a similar technique. At the conclusion of his song 'Axis: Bold as Love', Hendrix's producer Eddie Kramer introduced a technique called 'flanging', where the sound material is sent simultaneously to two tape recorders in record mode. The tape engineer then places a finger on the flange of the take-up reel of one of the recorders. This creates a very small delay between the two machines and the resulting sound is that of a jet, rushing and swirling. Kramer recalls:

We were experimenting with stereo flanging/phasing and demonstrated this for the first time to Jimi during a playback of 'Axis: Bold as Love.' He collapsed on the floor holding his head in his hands shouting 'Oh man how did you do that?' I heard that sound in my dreams . . . play it again . . . wow, wow. I want that sound on everything man![34]

Brian Eno's extraordinary 1978 album *Music for Airports* includes a piece made entirely of tape loops. '2/1' is comprised of seven tape loops of different lengths between approximately 17 and 31 seconds. Each loop has, somewhere in the middle, a five-second note sung in unison by three women singers and the composer. Eno deliberately avoided measuring the tape loops. He simply estimated what would be an adequate amount to make each loop, never intending them to be the same length.

According to Eno, one of the longer loops was 'running around a series of tubular aluminum chairs in Conny Plank's studio'.[35] 'And then I started all the loops running, and let them configure in the way they chose to configure. So sometimes you get dense clusters and fairly long silences, and then you get a sequence of notes that makes a kind of melody.'[36]

Eno's '2/1' is an example of what Michael Nyman calls 'electronic process' pieces, a class of compositions which 'specify a particular electronic system, which may in itself be inherently indeterminate and may or may not include a score for acting within its "electronic instrumentation"'.[37] Thus the electronic process piece itself might utilize a synthesizer patch, circuit diagram or, as in the case of '2/1', a plan for a set of interconnected pieces of equipment with instructions for performance.

Another good example of an electronic process piece that brings together performers and a particular electronic system is Gavin Bryars's 1971 composition 1, 2, 1-2-3-4. There are several versions of the piece, but one involves a group of instrumentalists and vocalists who each wear headphones connected to their own cassette machine. Each player hears only their 'part' on the tape. There is a count-off – '1, 2, 1-2-3-4' – and everyone starts their machine on the next downbeat. The performers attempt to play along with their part on the cassette tape. Because the cassette machines do not run at the exact same speed, the music does not start at exactly the same point on each tape and the performers themselves will have varying skill at imitating their parts, the musical material, although 'homogenous', begins to exhibit 'dislocations'.[38] It is precisely this musical drift that creates the music of Bryars's piece, in this case relying on the vicissitudes of the low-tech electronic system the composer specified.

Multi-track Tape Composition

Rock musicians and others quickly gravitated to the new ideas of tape music composition. In 1964 a little-known guitarist who had become fascinated with the music of Varèse, Frank Zappa, bought a small recording studio in Cucamonga, California, for $1,000. He renamed it Studio Z. The previous owner had custom-built a five-track tape recorder, giving Zappa his first access to multi-track recording. After his divorce, Zappa moved into the studio, 'beginning a life of obsessive overdubbage – non-stop, twelve hours a day'.[39] Recording became his daily compositional practice. Even after the notoriety and success of their first commercial album, *Freak Out!*, Zappa extended his recording practice to record his band, The Mothers of Invention, on a professional tape recorder whenever they performed out on the road. By the time he disbanded the Mothers, Zappa had collected enough recorded material for many albums.

Zappa's masterpiece, *Uncle Meat*, was produced between 1967 and 1969. It was recorded on a twelve-track recorder. Zappa includes careful notes about the studio gear in his liner notes, revealing the compositional status of the recording process for this music:

> The music on this album was recorded over a period of about 5 months from October 1967 to February 1968. Things that sound like a full orchestra were carefully assembled track by track through a procedure known as over-dubbing. The weird middle section of Dog Breath (after the line, 'Ready to attack') has forty tracks built into it. Things that sound like trumpets are actually clarinets played through an electric device made

by Maestro with a setting labeled Oboe D'Amore and sped up a minor third with a v.s.o. (variable speed oscillator). Other peculiar sounds were made on a Kalamazoo electric organ. The only equipment at our disposal for the modification of these primary sounds was a pair of Pultec Filters, two Lang Equalizers, and three Melchor Compressors built into the board at Apostolic Studios in New York. The board itself is exceptionally quiet and efficient (the only thing that allowed us to pile up so many tracks) and is the product of Mr. Lou Lindauer's imagination & workmanship. The material was recorded on a prototype Scully 12 track machine at 30 ips.[40]

The music of this album is an extraordinary flow of serene chamber music, 1950s rock, strange conversations, fragments of earlier live performances by the Mothers and highly abstract electronic passages. Most of the music was made by multiple overdubbing, speed changes on the recorder and many, many tape edits. Zappa's brilliant political interventions into 1950s and '60s pop music and culture, his ability to assemble eclectic musical material and his genius for montage and juxtaposition could not have been realized without the compositional possibilities of the multi-track recorder.

The Beatles and George Martin

The Beatles' *Sgt. Pepper's Lonely Hearts Club Band*, clearly one of the greatest rock albums ever made, was never destined for live performance. Released in 1967, it gave credence to the claim that there were really five Beatles, including the brilliant virtuoso producer George Martin. The album was composed in the studio. 'Strawberry Fields Forever' is, in fact, a juxtaposition of two different versions of the song, John Lennon having decided that he liked the first half of one version and the second half of the other. It happened that the two versions were keyed a semitone apart. Martin, using a variable-speed tape recorder, sped one version up by a quarter-tone and slowed the other down a quarter-tone, then joined them together.[41]

There is a fascinating fragment of *musique concrète* on the song 'Being for the Benefit of Mr Kite'. After the group laid down the basic tracks, Martin created a whole section of sound to suggest a circus soundscape. After collecting a group of old recordings of steam organs, Martin had sections transferred to tape. He then told the recording engineer to cut the tape into sections approximately 1 ft (30 cm) long. He asked the engineer to throw them up in the air, pick them up off the floor and splice them back together in whatever order he picked them up. Of course, some of the splices were backwards, and some were forwards.

> After he had laboriously stuck them all together again, we played the tape and I said: 'That piece there's a bit too much like the original. Turn it round the other way, backwards.' We went on like that until the tape was an amalgam of carousel noises . . . composed of fragments of tunes connected in a series of fractions of a second.[42]

A fully composed piece of *musique concrète* is found, of course, on the Beatles' *White Album*. Primarily John Lennon's creation, 'Revolution 9' is an eight-and-a-half-minute tape composition using all of the techniques developed by the classical avant-garde composers. The source material included Lennon and Yoko Ono talking and screaming, pianos, chaotic jamming, found sound, fragments of classical music recordings and bits from sound-effects records. The track comprises massive amounts of Schaefferian tape editing, many loops, overdubbing, reverberation and feedback.

In a Silent Way

Miles Davis's 1969 recording *In a Silent Way* is both famous and infamous. It is infamous for those who saw it as a sellout to rock music, not really jazz, and even boring. It is famous in the minds of those who heard the ethereal, minimalist, pulse-based music on side one, 'Shhh/Peaceful', as a whole new music. Davis must have known what would happen. Shortly before its release, he told critic Don Heckman, 'This one will scare the shit out of them.'[43]

Miles Davis must have also known that Teo Macero's bold use of tape editing on the album would be scandalous. Macero has said that the initial session, which produced forty reels of eight-track tape, had left the musicians unenthused. Joe Zawinul, who had composed the title track for the session, went so far as to say that he felt the musicians were 'noodling around'. Macero took the forty reels down to just two, one of eight-and-a-half minutes and the other just nine minutes. Miles came in to listen and Macero says that 'Davis got up and said "that's my record" and wouldn't budge.'[44] So, each side of the album, 'Shhh/Peaceful' and 'In a Silent Way', contained the unapologetic use of verbatim repeated sections of improvised music. Macero took what he had and, 'like cutting into the body',[45] 'composed out' each reel to make an album-length piece of music. 'Shhh/Peaceful' was a simple binary form, A-B-A, with the second A section being a tape-copy of the first A section. Some listeners even thought that it must have been a production mistake.

It was anything but a mistake. In fact, Macero had so transformed the music that a few weeks later Joe Zawinul, 'while passing a reception desk at CBS . . . asked the receptionist what the music playing was. "Why that's you and Miles and all the guys" . . . and it was really beautiful, you know?'[46]

In earlier recording sessions, such as the one for *Kind of Blue*, for example, Miles had been known to bring in brand new, unrehearsed material to his musicians. His musical relationship with Macero was similar, very spontaneous and improvisatory. As Davis began incorporating electronic instruments into his music, Macero and the recording studio itself would be brought even more directly into the trumpeter's compositional process.

In a Silent Way was truly a new music. It adumbrates the pulse-based, neo-tonal music of the ECM's northern Nordic jazz musicians, jazz fusion and ambient music.

Tubular Bells

Mike Oldfield's *Tubular Bells* (1973) is an important example of the power of the multi-track recorder as a compositional tool in rock music. Written and performed entirely by a shy young guitarist on a multi-track recorder at Virgin Records' country studio, The Manor, *Tubular Bells* became a worldwide hit in a matter of months after its release. Oldfield describes making the demo of *Tubular Bells* in his room:

> Well, I had a Bang and Olufsen with a sound on sound facility . . . you know, a bit like track jumping. Anyway, I did a bit in mono which meant that I ended up with half the instruments on one side of the tape. Then it had this strange button which said 'overdub' which, when you pressed it, allowed you to put one instrument on the other side. I blocked off the erase head with a piece of cardboard and then superimposed on that side until I ended up with both sides full and nothing in the middle. The only instruments I had were an electric organ borrowed from the band I was in and electric lead and bass guitars.[47]

Oldfield and his two engineers, Tom Newman and Simon Heyworth, spent many hours composing the broadly outlined piece right at the sixteen-track recorder. Newman recalls:

> We put the glockenspiel down . . . all the way through. We put a lot of that on until it seemed like long enough. Then we put the piano part on top of that, then he [Oldfield] played the bass part on that. We built it up like that and just kept it going until it felt like it ought to change. Then we would drop something else in on top of that and rub the rest of the track out [erase it] at the point when we felt it ought to change. Then we started the next bit . . .[48]

One critical response captures well the new compositional technique of tape music that Schaeffer had envisioned, that is, bypassing musical notation:

> Oldfield himself plays most of the instrumental parts that make up the sound fabric of his three tone-poems (chiefly a vast array of guitars, keyboard instruments and synthesizers) . . . The real subtlety of his music rarely lies in its actual material, but in the way the material is presented. In a long laborious process, he creates his music by recording it directly onto tape, over-dubbing track on track, until he arrives at the desired whole. (Like the Impressionists, texture is a prime element for him.) There can be no question: this is definitely a valid form of musical composition – the composer has total control over the completed entity.[49]

Oldfield talked about this music in terms of its 'textures'. His descriptions reveal a concern with layering tracks to create electronic orchestrations of musical ideas. He describes techniques such as recording between twenty and thirty guitars and electric basses played in melodic unison, then sub-mixing them to a single track. Elsewhere he describes tracking six electric guitars played in harmony to build up organ-like chords.[50]

Oldfield took multi-track composition to the extreme to produce a music that encompasses folk music, progressive rock and English pastoral music, and many, if not most, rock artists quickly adopted this new way of creating music. More importantly, new musical genres arose that were *entirely* studio-based, such as Zouk music in the French Antilles, Jamaican Dub, pioneered by 'King Tubby' and Lee 'Scratch' Perry, and synthesized classical music realizations by Wendy Carlos, Patrick Gleason and Isao Tomita.

In retrospect, the development of the tape recorder was as important to modern musical thinking as the adoption of equal temperament was to the development of the tonal system. Thinking analogically, the tape recorder became a musical instrument. It also became a sonic canvas on which musicians could compose as if it were score paper. Music notation was no longer necessary to compose music. Interestingly, even the tape recorder's transport controls – play, record, pause, stop, rewind – are modelled today in virtually all of the latest digital recording and composition software tools. The representation of a compositional 'timeline' in these programs is effectively like looking at a reel of recording tape and seeing the waveforms as a scroll of sounds.

In terms of musical practice, the use of magnetic tape as a storage medium allowed a vast new range of creative interventions. The origins of musical composition expanded as the memory or traces of previous sound events became available for re-composition. Editing magnetic tape permitted the alteration of musical time itself because composers could reposition, remove, or repeat sound events. And, as the practice developed, composers fractured recorded sounds themselves, changed the speed and direction of sounds, created echoes and loops, and even layered and juxtaposed different performances from one recording session to the next. For composers and performers, the tape record took off like a musical time machine, propelling musical culture into multiple sonic dimensions.

Wendy Carlos posed with a Moog synthesizer, 1968.

2
CIRCUITS

In 1931 the French composer Edgard Varèse completed *Ionisation*, the first Western classical composition scored exclusively for percussion instruments. Frank Zappa liked to say that this piece inspired him to become a composer. Among the forty instruments called for in the score were two hand-cranked sirens. These siren sounds within *Ionisation* have often been misunderstood. Some writers invoked the work of the Italian Futurists and their Noise Machines (Intonarumori) and suggested that the piece was about the sounds and dynamism of the city. In fact, Varèse was attempting to realize something much more abstract: 'I have always felt the need of a kind of continuous flowing curve that [conventional] instruments could not give me. That is why I used sirens in several of my works.'[1] This and many other sonic imaginings are why Varèse has been credited with envisioning the electronic medium well before the technology existed for modern electroacoustic music.

John Cage's 1939 composition *Imaginary Landscape No. 1* is another example of a composer's search for new, pure tones. The piece is scored for two variable-speed turntables, recordings, piano and cymbal:

> I used continuous sounds that were made for test purposes
> by the [RCA] Victor Company, and they had both constant
> tones and tones that were constantly sliding in pitch through
> a whole range.[2]

Radio technicians, laboratory technicians and public address operators used 'test records'. An oscillator produced the variety of tones on these records electronically. They were never intended as musical sources, yet Cage heard in them something that would later become the basic sonic material for electronic music.

In 1956 Bebe and Louis Barron created the first all-electronic music soundtrack for a Hollywood film, the science-fiction classic *Forbidden Planet*. Bebe Barron was a trained composer who organized the sounds using traditional tape techniques, while her husband built the circuits to create the sounds. These were not just any circuits. Louis had read Norbert Weiner's 1948 book *Cybernetics: Or Control and Communication in the Animal and the Machine* and used Weiner's ideas to design circuits that had a built-in lifespan, after which they would burn out and fail. Writer Anaïs Nin was a friend of the couple and wrote about her experience with them in one of her diaries, noting that 'The Barrons make their music with electrons, which they activate to create circuits. In fact, Louis' talk was full of circuits.'[3] Nin goes on to record a conversation she had with Louis, who explained:

> The circuits are our actors . . . We set them up in a dramatic
> situation in relation to each other and then we stimulate them
> to behave in accordance with it; start with some provocation
> to make them fight or make love or whatever . . . Sound is
> produced by the behavior of the electrons in these circuits . . . If
> left to their own behavior they will do what come natural [sic]
> to them. But they need prodding . . . Each circuit, as I say, has a

tendency to do something, though it may rebel against instructions: When it does we have to knock it around electronically
... What we have is a new artistic tool: direct communication
by pure emotion rather than by a symbol which must be
retranslated in the mind.[4]

To 'stimulate' these circuits, Louis would intervene directly
in the circuit path, changing a resistance or capacitance, or
creating some kind of feedback loop. When Nin said that this
sounded like 'cybernetics', she writes that Barron responded:

Precisely. Well, science has been borrowing from nature and
the arts to prove its theories, so why shouldn't artists borrow
the tools of science to express emotional ideas? What is
evolving is a new art form, completely electronic.[5]

What made Louis Barron's idea of a 'completely electronic'
art possible was the vacuum tube (valve), invented in 1909 by
Lee De Forest. First to come was the audio amplifier. Much like
the transformative nature of the tape recorder, the amplification
of sound creates the possibility of new dynamic relationships
with the listener. Tube technology was also responsible for the
development of the audio oscillator in the 1920s. The oscillator
could produce periodic vibrations and was used initially in radio
transmission. In the 1960s the transistor replaced the vacuum
tube as the basic building block of amplifiers and oscillators.

Electronic oscillators – tube or transistor – usually produce
a sine or a square wave. Sine waves are 'pure tones', that is,
fundamental vibrations without overtones. Sine waves do
not exist in the natural sound world. This smooth, periodic
oscillation held a particular interest because of the work of the
French mathematician Joseph Fourier, who proved that any
complex vibration is comprised of a fundamental frequency and

its constituent overtones (harmonics) that can be expressed as a sum of a series of sine waves.

For many composers involved in electronic music at this time, Fourier's fascination with the mathematics of sound waves became their fascination as well. This concept suggested to them that if any natural sound could be analysed as the sum of a series of sine waves, then new, previously unheard sounds could be created by applying the technique in reverse – that is, sounds could be constructed from scratch by superimposing sine waves of different frequencies. This exciting technique later became known as 'additive synthesis'.

Additive synthesis implied a radial shift away from Pierre Schaeffer's *musique concrète* techniques that relied on recorded natural sounds. More than a simple difference of taste, a cultural and ideological rift developed that could be seen as geographic: Paris or Cologne.

Karlheinz Stockhausen was the pivotal figure in advancing the use of electronically produced sounds to build musical compositions. It is his name and reputation that is most closely associated with *elektronische Musik*.[6] Stockhausen had produced his *Konkrete Etüde* at Schaeffer's Paris studio in 1952, but he was eager to leave Paris for Cologne to work at the recently formed electronic music studio at the Nordwestdeutscher Rundfunk (Northwest German Broadcasting Station, NWDR), in large part because he was unhappy working with only recorded sound sources. In a letter to his friend Karel Goeyvaerts he wrote:

> We shall use electronic sound production in the future . . . and we shall govern the material; it won't govern us. 'Musique concrète' – I sensed this from the first day, is nothing but capitulation before the undefined, a terribly dilettantish gamble, uncontrolled improvisation.[7]

In retrospect, this seems a rigid artistic stance. Nowadays, many electronic music composers would revel in the risks of 'uncontrolled improvisation'. In the context of Stockhausen's creative polemic, Cage's silent piece, 4′33″, would exemplify an existential capitulation to the world of ambient sound. Nonetheless, this dialectic was extremely productive, and informed many of the theoretically uncompromising compositions that are associated with Stockhausen's music at this time.

Composer and theorist Herbert Eimert and physicist and acoustician Werner Meyer-Eppler had established the studio in 1951. They promoted it as the first studio of its kind 'to produce the new musical material [that is, electronically produced sounds] and to study the problems of its production and processing systematically'.[8] Critical here is the notion of 'systematic study'. In contrast to Schaeffer's *Treatise on Musical Objects* (1966), which was really a study of sonic phenomenology, NWDR published 'technical papers' on electronic sound that included detailed descriptions of studio equipment, circuit schematics and electronic music terminology.

The extraordinary confluence of technology and analytics at the Cologne studio inspired and reinforced Stockhausen's rigorous aesthetic. By 1954 Stockhausen had completed *Electronic Study No. 1* and *Electronic Study No. 2*. Each of these highly abstract works focused on additive sine-wave constructions that he called 'tone mixtures'. The pieces are serially organized, that is, all musical parameters are directly related to each other. In the case of *Electronic Study No. 1*, everything stems from a group of 'just' interval ratios. In *Electronic Study No. 2*, everything is derived from the number five. The pieces are thus the first electronic compositions to systematically compose musical timbres.

Additive synthesis would remain only partially attainable until the era of digital sound synthesis. With only a small number of oscillators available in the NWDR studio, Stockhausen may have felt it necessary to incorporate *musique concrète* techniques into his new *Gesang der Jünglinge* (Song of the Youths, 1956). Whatever his reasons, this work is an early masterpiece of electronic music. Using recordings of a boy soprano reading texts from the Book of Daniel, Stockhausen created a music that was generated by the pitch content of the boy's voice. He matched the formants, the regions of resonance that occur because of the resonant qualities of the vocal and nasal cavities, with electronic sounds built from sine waves. The non-pitched part of the speech was matched by electronically generated noise and impulses. The piece was originally composed with five channels of sound, as the composer was very interested in the notion of spatialized music.

Two years later, Stockhausen went on to produce another masterwork, *Kontakte* (1958). A quadraphonic composition, it explores the pulse wave as a generator of both pitch and rhythm, massive noise textures and the composer's ongoing interest in sound spatialization. Stockhausen invented a spinning speaker that had four microphones every ninety degrees. Sounds could be sent to the speaker and then re-recorded as they moved in space.[9]

Although Stockhausen did not employ them in his *Electronic Study Nos.* 1 and 2, the NWDR studio had a Trautonium and a Melochord, two rudimentary electronic instruments using oscillators. The Trautonium did not have a conventional keyboard but used a length of metal. Pressure on the metal controlled amplitude, while pitch change was the result of sliding a finger along its length. In contrast to the Trautonium, the Melochord, invented by Harald Bode, did have a conventional keyboard that was switchable from a three- to a seven-octave range. A foot pedal controlled amplitude and there was envelope control. A later version even provided rudimentary timbral control. So, in one sense, these were early prototypes of synthesizers. It was, however, the RCA Corporation that could truly claim to have built the first modern synthesizer.

In the 1940s Harry F. Olson, a senior technician at RCA who was an expert in acoustics, turned his attention to the idea of creating electronic musical sound. By 1951 Olson and a colleague, Herbert Belar, had designed and built the RCA Mark I Synthesizer. The machine was room-sized because it used vacuum tube (valve) technology. It had twelve oscillators and was capable of four-voice polyphony. The Mark II version had 24 oscillators and provided enveloped control, noise generators, high- and low-pass filters, low-frequency modulation and portamento. Until 1959 the sounds were recoded direct to disc on a cutting lathe, just as Schaeffer did in his Paris studio.

The RCA synthesizer is important for two reasons. First, the circuitry of the synthesizer itself was analogue – using tube technology – and was modular in design. Second, the Mark II RCA synthesizer was controlled by what amounted to player piano rolls, a fascinating early example of digital control. This is a critical factor in the history of electronic music, because it adumbrates the digital control that was to come twenty years later, particularly the MIDI protocol. Here, as in many instances in the history of electronic music, there have never been clear boundaries between analogue and digital technologies. With its large number of oscillators, the RCA synthesizer brought composers a little closer to true additive synthesis. Third, its modular design, requiring the connections to be made by 'patch cords', formed the model for the transistor-based synthesizer designs such as Moog, Buchla and Arp that appeared about ten years later.

In 1957 the powerful Mark II RCA synthesizer was given to the Columbia-Princeton Electronic Studio in New York City. For the first time, Babbitt was able to access an instrument capable of playing his intricate 1961 work *Composition for Synthesizer*. Babbitt's piece is a serial composition using twelve-tone rows that have been mapped into rhythms. The time-point set is derived from the interval relationships of a particular row form, so that an interval separated by nine half-steps will generate a duration of nine metric pulses. This creates quite complex rhythms, but ones that Babbitt was able to program precisely into the RCA synthesizer via its punched paper rolls. The different timbres Babbitt created with the synthesizer do much to bring into relief the melodies and chords generated by the simultaneous use of the various forms of the row.

All of Babbitt's electronic works were realized on the RCA Synthesizer. For about ten years it was the only machine of its kind, and Babbitt was willing to spend the long hours necessary to program it. The complex pitch relationships and rhythms of Babbitt's music were well suited to the instrument, and he remained the only composer to use it extensively.

When the transistor began to be commercially available in the 1960s, its bulky tube technology made the RCA synthesizer a dinosaur. The transistor was small and powerful, and it began to replace the vacuum tube. This completely transformed electronics design and production. Whereas the RCA synthesizer took up an entire room, the coming transistor-based synthesizer designs would fit into a pair of large suitcases.

The Moog Synthesizer

In the late 1950s a Cornell University student named Robert Moog was dividing his time between his studies and his cottage industry of making and selling Theremins, the instrument invented in the 1920s in Russia by Léon Theremin. The instrument has two antennae that respond to the position of the player's hands, one controlling the pitch, the other loudness. The player never touches the antennae, but brings the hands in proximity to them. Theremins are very expressive as a result of these subtle hand movements. The most famous Thereminist was Clara Rockmore, who performed widely during the 1930s. Moog had become obsessed with the instrument in high school, and had developed a process of making and selling the kits. In 1963 he decided to expand his business and rented a storefront in Trumansburg, New York, a few miles from Cornell.

Herbert Deutsch, a musician who taught at Hofstra University, owned one of Moog's Theremins. In what was to be a fortuitous and historic conversation, Deutsch described to Moog the new field of electronic music. Moog, so focused on his obsession with the inner workings of the Theremin, was completely unaware of the cultural developments outside his sphere. Their friendship quickly developed into a collaboration. Almost immediately, they began to discuss the idea of a portable electronic music device. Moog first showed Deutsch a way to control the frequency of an oscillator by applying a voltage to it, rather than just turning a knob by hand. Deutsch realized that the concept of 'voltage control' was revolutionary because it set the synthesizer on a course to make it much more of a musical instrument, not a traditional one, but one that was modulation-centred. This included developing keyboard control, and eventually Moog, modifying an old electronic organ, was able to trigger a pitch and a time-shape for each note, now known as an 'envelope'.

Their collaboration led to more sophisticated oscillators that could generate various waveforms, filters and envelope generators – separate modules that 'talk' to each other via voltage control. The concept of a reasonably portable 'modular synthesizer' was taking shape, largely owing to the transistor circuitry Moog was utilizing in his designs.

At roughly the same time but quite independently, Ramon Sender and Morton Subotnick, composers at the San Francisco Tape Music Center, began collaborating with electronics wizard Donald Buchla on a synthesizer. Called the Buchla Box, the device employed the same ideas that had occurred to Moog. Buchla remarked:

> I had this idea you could take voltages and multiply and mix them and things like that. So it wasn't too far a cry for me to attach a voltage to the pitch of an oscillator or to the amplitude of a VCA [voltage-controlled amplifier] . . . But as soon as I added voltage control to the elements of the synthesizer it became a different ball game because you could parametize everything. You weren't limited by how fast you could turn a knob to get between two states of a parameter.[10]

This idea of voltage control was by far the most forward-looking aspect of the nascent modular synthesizer. Voltage control was really compositional control. The flow of control voltage largely determined what a particular patch could do, musically speaking.

The Analogue Synthesizer

The architecture of the modern modular synthesizer began to be conceptualized as a collection of three things: sound sources, sound modifiers and amplifiers. In this signal flow, the 'amplifiers' were specialized in that they could be turned on and off in order to create a time-shape or note event. Each section – whether sound sources, modifiers or amplifiers – could be addressed with control voltages. These control voltages could come from any module because every module used the same voltage range. It was the case that a module could be used to produce a control voltage in one patch and be used as an audio signal in another patch. The final requirement for the modular synthesizer was a system for amplifying and recording the resulting synthesized sound.

Sound sources are oscillators which produce periodic vibrations that we hear as pitched sound, that is, a fundamental frequency and – except for the sine wave – harmonic components or overtones. The modular synthesizer oscillator usually produced one or more of the following types of periodic vibrations: a sine wave, which is a fundamental only with no overtones; a triangle wave, which has a fundamental and relatively low-amplitude harmonics; a sawtooth wave, which consists of a fundamental and fairly loud harmonics; and a pulse wave, which has a fundamental and changeable harmonic content.

Unlike the three previous continuously varying wave shapes, the pulse wave is unique in that it is either on or off. The ratio of the on-time to the off-time will determine which harmonics are present. A special variety of the pulse wave that is equally on and off is called a square wave. The square wave is comprised of a fundamental, and strong, odd-numbered partials.

The noise generator is a sound source that produces a random mixture of all audible frequencies, analogous to white light, which is a random mixture of all visible frequencies of light. Noise can be 'weighted' towards certain ranges. For example, white noise is weighted towards higher random frequencies, while pink noise is balanced across the audible spectrum.

Filters are the primary signal modifiers in modular synthesizers. A filter is an electronic circuit that will pass a specific band of frequencies while attenuating others. The four common types of filters are low-pass, high-pass, band-pass and band-reject filters. In the case of the low-pass filter, the circuit passes signals with a frequency lower than an adjustable cut-off frequency, and attenuates signals with frequencies higher than the cut-off frequency. The high-pass filter does the opposite, passing frequencies about its cut-off frequency and attenuating frequencies below it. The band-pass filter is a circuit that passes signals *between* two specific frequencies, but that attenuates the signals above and below. Finally, the band-reject filter passes most frequencies, but attenuates those between two specific frequencies.

Using filters in modular synthesis is known as subtractive synthesis, where the filter literally sculpts the sound by removing part of it. This simple but powerful technique remains one of the most common ways to shape sounds.

Another important sound modifier is the ring modulator. The ring modulator has two inputs and one output. The inputs are usually two oscillators or an oscillator and an audio source such as a microphone, electric musical instrument or other audio signal. The ring modulator produces the sum and difference of the frequencies of the two inputs. The result is quite unpredictable, but is often bell-like in its sound quality.

We must, of course, include the synthesizer keyboard as a sound modifier, as it is most often used to shift the frequency of the oscillators up and down. Synthesizer keyboards are quantized, meaning that the pitch relationship they produce from the oscillators is usually equal-tempered, mimicking the relationships on a traditional piano or organ. However, many keyboard controllers could be adjusted for other temperaments. In the case of the early synthesizers, the keyboard was monophonic, producing only one note at a time.

Moog and Buchla also produced a ribbon controller, a device that was played by moving a finger along a metal ribbon. If connected to an oscillator, it would provide subtle pitch inflections and glissandi. Most synthesizer keyboards could also produce a portamento, that is, a slide between one key and the next when playing the keyboard.

Amplifiers comprise the third section of synthesizer architecture. However, there are specialized ones – called 'voltage-controlled amplifiers' – that are used to produce 'note events'. A note event is a sound that has some kind of easily perceived start, middle and end in real time. In a synthesizer, note events are usually produced by a combination of an envelope generator and a voltage-controlled amplifier. Recall that in classic tape music composition, note events had to be created by splicing silence before and after a sound. This module pairing within the synthesizer architecture changed everything, eliminating that time-consuming aspect of traditional tape composition.

More precisely, each module of this pairing did a specific job: the envelope generator specified the start, middle and end-time of a note event; it was connected to a voltage-controlled amplifier that would turn on and off according to the voltage shape fed to it. A single note event would result when the envelope generator was triggered, just as when a musician would pluck a string or sing a note.

It was one of the directors of the Columbia-Princeton Electronic Music Studio, Vladimir Ussachevsky, collaborating with Robert Moog on his early modules, who conceptualized the idea of the micro-evolution of a note event. Ussachevsky generalized the acoustic sound event, calling the sections the 'attack, initial decay, sustain, and release', shortened to ADSR.

The signal flow on a synthesizer is relatively complex in that the composer must route a signal path (the sound itself) and a control path (a set of voltage connections to trigger the sound and modify it) in order to create a sound. In a certain sense, these signal and control paths, of which there are seemingly endless variations, become a new kind of musical score.

The Composer and the Synthesizer

If composers played a major role in the development of the analogue modular synthesizer, its future was also in the hands of performers who played a large part in moving the synthesizer from the laboratory to the stage and recording studio, not to mention into the public eye. By the late 1960s there seemed to be no limit to the musical possibilities of this new instrument.

If there is one popular work that marked the entry of the synthesizer into the realm of musical instruments, it was Wendy Carlos's 1968 record *Switched-on Bach*, an international phenomenon played over and over on the airwaves and in homes. The record contained realizations of selected works of J. S. Bach, painstakingly multi-tracked by Carlos and producer Rachel Elkind. The record, one of the best-selling classical records at the time, made Carlos a superstar and the Moog a thing of wonder. In addition to receiving three Grammy awards that year, Glenn Gould, a classical superstar himself, called the version of Bach's 'Brandenburg' Concerto No. 4 on her next record *The Well-tempered Synthesizer*, the best performance of the piece that he had ever heard.

Wendy Carlos was a musician and recording engineer who made important contributions to the development of the first production model of the Moog. For example, Carlos was instrumental in making the keyboard more usable by holding that last note played. She also gave him the idea for a portamento option on the keyboard, sliding between the first and next notes played.

While Carlos remains, perhaps, the most well-known synthesist, there are many composers and performers who were part of this exploding genre. They came from many different musical spheres.

Keith Emerson was a self-taught organist who consistently gravitated towards classical music for inspiration. His music with the group the Nice, particularly their album *Five Bridges Suite*, really set the stage for the classical music influences that created the sound of progressive rock bands like King Crimson, Yes, Genesis and Gentle Giant. Carlos's *Switched-on Bach* was a revelation to Emerson:

> With the Moog, I went to a record shop where they knew me . . . They played it for me in the shop. I didn't honestly like it. The guy played it for me because it had the Brandenburg thing in G which I had done with the Nice [on *Ars Longa Vita Brevis*] . . . But there was this picture of the thing it was played on, and I said, 'So what's this?' And he said it was like a telephone switchboard. And I said, 'Oh that's interesting.' So I bought the album. I got word through my office that a guy by the name of Mike Vickers had had a Moog shipped over to England, so I asked if I could have a look at it. We got together, and he set it up in his room. He explained to me the functioning of the instrument. I said, 'Well, can it be used on stage?' And he said, 'No way. You don't realize the complications in this. There's no way you could do that.' I thought there must be some way, and asked, 'What if you hid down behind this thing and programmed it while I was playing it? You know, set us all these things and keep it in tune?' I was playing at the Festival Hall with the Royal Philharmonic and the Nice . . . So Mike Vickers was hunched down backstage, but he'd pop up every now and then and put a plug in somewhere. It worked excellently. So, I immediately sent off to Moog and got some literature back . . .
>
> It arrived in a box, no instructions or anything. It was all in bits and pieces. I couldn't even get a sound out of it. I was at the point of throwing the damn thing out the window. I frantically

> rang up Mike Vickers and asked him, 'How do I get a sound
> here?' ... He knew how to operate his unit, but it had taken
> him ages because he hadn't gotten any instructions either ...
> He came over with diagrams to show me which switches were
> envelope generators, and which were the voltage-controlled
> amplifiers, and which were the mixers, and so on ...[11]

Emerson, having mastered the modular Moog as a solo
melodic instrument with his group Emerson, Lake and Palmer,
showcased his large Moog synthesizer to millions of rock fans.

In the jazz realm, Annette Peacock and Paul Bley represent
a very interesting part of this history, apart from the more
mainstream and commercial users of the Moog in the early
years after its development. Two of the most important
innovators of avant-garde jazz and improvised music, they were
at first unaware of the Moog. Peacock relates that she and Bley
were visiting pop critic Don Heckman. Heckman played them
some of Carlos's *Switched-on Bach*.

> I fell right in love with it; it was the first new instrument in
> three hundred years ... on the way over to see Robert Moog I
> psyched out exactly the tack to take with him in terms of inter-
> esting him in giving us a synthesizer because we didn't have
> any money. So Paul said, 'We've got to take the synthesizer
> away; if we don't take it away with us then we won't get it,'
> so we went over in the station wagon. We got out all of Paul's
> publicity and press and went over there. We thought that
> Walter [Wendy] Carlos was getting a lot of attention and credit
> and we felt that as Robert Moog had invented the instrument
> he might like a little bit of it himself. So we took the tack that
> we were going to create music with it rather than just use it as
> a 'jingle'-type instrument and we were going to incorporate
> it into the main field of music, give it some dignity and the

> respect it deserves. So we went up there and Paul did the rap
> ... and we drove away that night with a synthesizer.[12]

Despite their initial enthusiasm, it actually took Peacock and
Bley quite a while to realize what they had promised Moog,
since they experienced many problems in using the large
synthesizer in live improvisation.

> We took it back to New York where nobody knew what a
> synthesizer was. Not only that, but anybody who did know
> what it was, or who had been working on it – the commercial
> people – wouldn't tell you anything about it, and there was no
> information about it. So we had this thing that looked like an
> aircraft cockpit and it was sitting in our bedroom ... Then we
> decided to set it up again and I started fooling around with it
> and patching. We had to make all these charts – I drew the way
> it looked and notated the patching so we could find the sounds
> again. I actually invented a way to graft the voice onto it.
>
> The first gig we did was at the Village Vanguard, and we had
> to make the audience wait twenty minutes between tunes
> while we changed the patching. It was ridiculous. Anyway, it
> went on from there. We toured Europe and carried the stuff
> around. The Europeans weren't very happy because they were
> used to Paul as an acoustic player ...
>
> Then my father died and left me five thousand dollars and I
> produced a concert at the Philharmonic Hall [December 1969]
> ... We did the first live concert with synthesizer and voice.[13]

Bley and Peacock made a record in 1971 documenting this
project called *Revenge*. In addition to Bley's brilliant playing, it
features electronically processed vocals by Annette Peacock.

The Buchla Synthesizer

Although it might seem that the brand of synthesizer would make only a minimal difference in compositional thinking, it is striking to compare the music produced on the Buchla synthesizer to that of the Moog. Shortly before Carlos's *Switched-on Bach*, composer Morton Subotnick had produced an album-length composition entitled *Silver Apples of the Moon* produced on a Buchla system. The work is almost jazz-like, with punchy, cascading melodies and complex rhythms. It has an improvised feel, due in large part to Buchla's unique controllers.

Don Buchla is famous for his metal touch keyboard, similar to the ribbon controller idea, but much more nuanced. In the model 112, touching a 'key' would produce two tunable voltages. Each key also produced a voltage proportional to finger pressure on the key. Additionally, each key touch would produce a pulse output that could be used to trigger a note event. Buchla described his device as kinaesthetic input ports:

> They were all capacitance-sensitive touch-plates, or resistance-sensitive in some cases, organized in various sorts of arrays . . . I saw no reason to borrow from a keyboard, which is a device invented to throw hammers at strings, later on, for operating switches for electronic organs and so-on. A keyboard is dictatorial. When you've got a black and white keyboard there it's hard to play anything but keyboard music – And when there's not a black and white keyboard you get into the knobs and the wires and the interconnections and timbres, and you get involved in many other aspects of the music, and it's a far more experimental way. It's appealing to fewer people but it's more exciting.[14]

Buchla had also produced a sequencer so that the composer could essentially program melodic loops, or loops of voltages to be used elsewhere on the synthesizer. Subotnick used it extensively in his *Silver Apples*. He describes his discoveries in using Buchla's sequencer:

> There were three voltage-controlled outputs for each stage. I used to cascade two sequencers so that they would run simultaneously, giving you six voltages per stage. One voltage would control pitch, another spatial location, the third amplitude. Then one, which was really clever, would control the pulse generator that was controlling the sequencer, so that you could determine the absolute rhythm. You could literally program a very complex rhythm over a long period of time, for example, by running five stages against thirteen.[15]

The key phrase here is 'a long period of time'. Subotnick's work represents a self-generating approach to programming the synthesizer. Because of his attachment to the self-generating possibilities of the Buchla system, Subotnick became identified with long, continuously evolving patches throughout his music.

When the young composer and improviser Pauline Oliveros was appointed director of the San Francisco Tape Music Center in 1966, she began working with one of Buchla's new systems. Despite her excitement at working with this new instrument, she was sceptical of the transistor technology and its particular sound:

> I plunged into learning to use the Buchla 100 series synthesizer. I felt the loss of the old tube oscillators, and it took some time for me to adapt to the coolness of transistor-generated sound. The oscillators also did not have the high-frequency range above [human] hearing like the tube oscillators.[16]

Oliveros's resistance to the Buchla sound is understandable, given the sonic parameters of her very successful earlier electronic works. Working in Toronto in 1966, for instance, Oliveros had created a composition entitled *I of IV*. The piece was made with twelve tube oscillators producing sine waves tuned above the range of human hearing, but tuned in close proximity and amplified. This technique, called heterodyning, produces a difference tone – a third, subjective tone whose frequency is the difference between the frequencies of the real tones. Perhaps because she was one of the rare women composers working in electronic music at the time, Oliveros remembers being accused of 'black art . . . the director disconnected line amplifiers to discourage my practices, declaring that signal generators are of no use above or below the audio range because you can't hear them'.[17]

Oliveros's large Buchla composition *Alien Bog* was composed at Mills College in Oakland after the San Francisco Tape Music Center was relocated there in 1967. She used her tape delay system with the Buchla 100 series synthesizer. Oliveros's piece is totally abstract in its form and content, but has a wonderful organic sense. Her predilection for high-frequency sounds and her use of tape delay seems to match perfectly with the sounds from outside her studio window. She recalled that she was 'deeply impressed by the sounds from the frog pond outside the studio window at Mills. I loved the accompaniment as I worked on my pieces. Though I never recorded the frogs, I was of course deeply influenced by their music.'[18]

Another California composer, less well known but important nonetheless, was Douglas Leedy. His 1971 triple LP *Entropical Paradise* was a landmark of self-generative music and ambient musical thinking. Leedy described his music, made with both Buchla and Moog systems, as not really music, but 'acoustical environmental "programming" which should be heard but not necessarily listened to'.[19] Each of the six pieces on the album are self-generating patches, that is, 'once programmed and set in motion . . . [they] could theoretically run continuously but without repetition indefinitely'.

Self-generating patches are now quite common in the music of the new generation of analogue modular synthesizer composers. Todd Barton calls his design the Krell patch as an homage to Bebe and Louis Barron's all-electronic soundtrack to the film *Forbidden Planet*. He writes:

My self-generating, ever-changing Krell patch owes its genesis to the magnificent generative Buchla patches of Douglas Leedy's *Entropical Paradise* . . . I'm guessing the roots of these patches can be traced back to Norbert Weiner's landmark book, *Cybernetics: Or Control and Communication in the Animal and the Machine*, in which he unfolds self-governing and modifying feedback systems. The core of the Krell patch is a self-cycling attack-decay envelope generator, which initially pumps out a steady stream of fast attack/fast decay envelopes. By sending different random, fluctuating or asynchronous control voltages to the attack and decay parameters, a new and unpredictable stream of diverse envelope shapes and asymmetrical rhythms unfolds: an unsuspected flurry of staccato riffs followed by slow, legato passages and silences and 'breaths.'[20]

Barton revises Varèse's famous quote: 'I dream of instruments obedient to my thought and which with their contribution of a whole new world of unsuspected sounds, will lend themselves to the exigencies of my inner rhythm.' But here, Barton reminds us that 'the "inner rhythm" and "thought" are coming from within the feedback loops of the circuitry itself!'

The connections between composers and designers shaped the continuing use and development of analogue synthesizers.

Peter Zinovieff's London-made EMS VCS-3 was released in 1969. Used by a wide range of composers and musicians from Delia Derbyshire to Brian Eno to Pink Floyd, the VCS-3 was extremely powerful for its size. It had three oscillators, a low-pass filter, ring modulator, reverb and two innovative design features. The first innovation was its pin-matrix patching, a two-dimensional grid where inserting a pin connected a particular row and column wired to the module inputs and outputs. The second was its 'joy-stick', a two-dimensional analogue grid outputting X and Y voltages. To this day, many composers and musicians claim that the VCS-3 is one of the best-sounding analogue synthesizers ever made.

Composer Jean-Michel Jarre composed *Oxygène* with a VCS-3, other analogue synthesizers and an eight-track recorder in the kitchen of his Paris apartment. Like Oldfield's *Tubular Bells*, it became a huge commercial success though there was little initial interest from record companies because of the lack of voice and lyrics. Jarre praised the EMS synthesizer:

> To me, the original VCS-3 synthesizer is like a Stradivarius . . . When I started out, this synth was my primary tool along with a Farfisa organ and two Revox recorders. Pink Floyd began using this synth around the same time, when they started introducing electronic elements to their music, but they used it as a secondary element in a rock arrangement – whereas for me, it was the primary tool in my sonic palette.[21]

The Minimoog is a monophonic analogue synthesizer that was released in 1970 by R. A. Moog Inc. It was designed in response to the use of synthesizers in rock and pop music. It had three oscillators, a mixer, a low-pass filter and a voltage-controlled amplifier. It was quite portable, included a small built-in keyboard and had pitch-bend and modulation wheels.

The Minimoog became a common sound on many recordings as a solo lead and bass-line instrument.

The most remarkable creative use of the Minimoog, however, is found on Sun Ra's 1970 recording *My Brother the Wind*. Sun Ra and his band visited the Moog factory in upstate New York the year before. Moog had lent Sun Ra a Minimoog prototype – never to be returned – and the composer immediately began using it in his performances. The musical fluency of Sun Ra's use of the Minimoog in these tracks is astonishing, and even more so because there was apparently no multi-tracking done in the session.

Pianist Joe Zawinul began using two Arp 2600 synthesizers with his jazz-fusion group Weather Report in 1971. The Arp 2600 also had three oscillators, but included more sound modifiers such as a ring modulator and reverb. It was designed for live performance. One could use patch cords, but most of the connections were hard-wired, and could be controlled on the fly by moving the faders in the middle of the panel. As to the sound, he said in an interview:

> I like the Arp because of what I can do with it. I hear the Moog, it's immediately the Moog. With the Arp I can do things that will fool the heck out of you. I can hide between the voices, I can do all kinds of things. To me it's a much more natural sound. The variety of colors is greater, too.[22]

In an Arp advertisement he even describes the differences between his two 2600s:

> I want orchestral sounds from a synthesizer, the kind of realism beyond imitation. I can make the 2600 sound like Coltrane, just like Coltrane . . . or change it to soft, haunting flutes. My first 2600, 'Eins,' is my soft synthesizer, with a clear, clean

sound I have never heard on any other. 'Zwei,' my second 2600, gives me a harder edge.[23]

Arp also made a large studio synthesizer, the model 2500. It has a famous place in Steven Spielberg's 1977 film *Close Encounters of the Third Kind*, where the 2500 is used to communicate with the aliens who have come to earth. It's most serious user, however, was the French composer Éliane Radigue, who composed with it exclusively. She composed with her Arp 2500, her ears and a stopwatch, trying to hear what each sound 'wanted' to be and how long it should last. Radigue also developed a scroll notation system to represent all of the modules of her synthesizer, their settings and durations. Her *Trilogie de la mort* (Trilogy on Death, 1998) is a deeply meditative and sonically challenging piece that lasts for almost three hours. It is clearly the most extensive piece ever written for the Arp 2500, and probably for any synthesizer. She describes her working process, going against many established narratives of composing:

> Another story was beginning. A story where breath, pulsations, beating, murmurs and above all the natural production of these marvelous, delicate and subtle harmonics could be deployed in a differently organized manner. No acceptable intervals to tolerate or obey. No harmonic progression. No recursion or inverted series, no respect for rules of atonality tending toward 'discordant.' Forget everything to learn again. The freedom to be immersed in the ambivalence of continuous modulation with the uncertainty of being and/or not being in this or that mode or tonality. The freedom to let yourself be overwhelmed, submerged in a continuous sound flow where perceptual acuity is heightened through the discovery of a certain slight beating, there in the background, pulsations, breath.[24]

Phase Two: Tangerine Dream, The Sequencer and Digitality

Tangerine Dream, a German avant-garde rock band heavily influenced by the music of Stockhausen, set the stage for the next era of analogue electronic music, one that quickly began to be influenced by emerging digital technology. In this case it was Robert Moog's sequencer that was responsible. The Moog 960 sequencer, then called a 'sequential controller', was one of the first step sequencers for electronic music. There were eight steps, each with three voltage outputs. A built-in clock (oscillator) stepped through each stage and could be set to repeat the pattern indefinitely. The control voltage outputs were usually used to tune a pitch setting on an oscillator, so a continually repeating riff or phrase was the most often heard result of a sequencer. Moog offered another module to accompany the 960, a sequential switch that would allow 24 stages instead of the normal eight.

It was Chris Franke who led the group toward its new sound: I didn't have a synth at the time of *Zeit*, but occasionally I would practice on the big Moog modular in the Hansa recording studios. They had got it inexpensively from The Rolling Stones, who used it for a film in 1967 and then saw no further use for it. Fricke and Eberhard Schoener were definitely the first people in Germany to own a Moog, and had paid 800,000 Marks each for the privilege! Anyway, nobody in Hansa knew how to use it. So I got involved, but wasn't allowed to take it out of the studio until 1973. It didn't have a user's manual, so for two years I kept rehearsing on it. Every night I'd go into the studio and explore the Moog with its bad patching and unstable sound. But what I discovered about it was the sequencing side, its ability to generate an ongoing rhythm. Its sound, to me, had analogies with the repetitive rhythms of Indian music. It wasn't boring,

so I just spent hours and hours creating sequences. Later,
Edgar heard it and thought its driving rhythm was perfect for
Tangerine Dream's music.[25]

Tangerine Dream's *Phaedra*, *Rubycon* and *Ricochet* provided
a new sonic resource for many areas of pop and dance music.
Their modal, drummer-less sequencer-driven grooves –
reminiscent of Terry Riley's 1969 recording *A Rainbow in Curved
Air* in which he used electric organ and tape loops to create a
driving, diatonic music – set the stage for Kraftwerk's *Trans-
Europe Express* and the work of producer Giorgio Moroder with
Donna Summer's 'I Feel Love' in 1977.

Kraftwerk used a custom-built sequencer called the
Synthanorma to drive their analogue synthesizers on *Trans-
Europe Express*. In the case of Moroder and Summer, 'I Feel Love'
was entirely created by a large Moog system with the exception
of the kick drum on the track:

> 'I Feel Love' was absolutely all done with the big one, the
> pieces of Moog all connected . . . There I was lucky because
> I had a great engineer, Robbie Wedel I think, who was able
> to get me a sound out. Because at that time you needed 12
> connections between oscillators and then every sound took
> like at least half an hour. Then I wanted to create sounds like
> the hi-hat, so we created a white noise, cut certain frequencies
> off, then the snare then some other percussion. Then, actually
> for that one I think I used one of the Italian synthesisers, which
> had already polyphonic stuff . . . The drums was all [Moog]
> except the bass drum. Because the Moog couldn't give me a
> punch sound, it would give me 'oomph' instead of 'dum.'[26]

The sound of sequenced musical lines, melodic phrases with
mechanistic rhythmic timing, and the mechanistic punch of

the drum machine began to fall together as the engine of dance music. It is still the sound of electronic dance music today.

Turn It Up!

Not surprisingly, merely *amplifying* traditional instruments had a profound effect on musical hearing, performance and composition. The history of the electric guitar is really the history of whole new genres of music. From the pump organ quietly playing hymns to the electrifying grooves of Jimmy Smith's Hammond B-3, amplification did not just make music louder, it made new music:

> We were doing a recording session with Miles and when I came into the studio I didn't see any acoustic piano anywhere . . . In the corner of the room was only this Wurlitzer electric piano that I'd never played before. I asked Miles what he wanted me to play, and he said 'Play that.' I was thinking 'That toy?' Then I turned it on and was really surprised by the sound. It sounded beautiful! . . . Miles was already listening to Jimi Hendrix and other rock artists . . .[27]

Herbie Hancock is speaking here of the 1968 recording session for Davis's *Miles in the Sky*. Hancock played an electric piano for the first time there on the tune 'Stuff', but it was the Fender-Rhodes electric piano that was to transform so much of jazz. Just a year later, the trumpeter used the Rhodes in full force on the *In a Silent Way* sessions.

The Fender-Rhodes has a fascinating history linked to the incapacities of the human body after war. In 1942 Harold Rhodes, a member of the U.S. Army Air Corps and former piano teacher, was tasked with providing lessons for wounded airmen. For bedridden soldiers, a full-size piano was out of the question so, using aluminium tubing salvaged from a B-17 aircraft, Rhodes produced a light and portable 29-note keyboard that used the tubes as tone generators, not unlike a set of wind chimes. This piano was known as the Army Air Corps Lap Model Piano. When the war ended he founded the Rhodes Piano Corporation.

Leo Fender bought Rhodes's company in 1959, and began producing the Piano Bass, a thirty-note keyboard (the lowest two-and-a-half octaves on a traditional piano). The Rhodes piano had a fairly traditional key and felt hammer mechanism, but that was where it ended. Here, the felted hammer struck a metal 'tine' which, after being set into vibration, was amplified by a small electromagnetic pickup (one for each note), similar to an electric guitar pickup. The tine was attached to a metal 'tone bar' that increased the sustain of each note.

The sound of this new instrument was more like a metallophone (for example, a vibraphone or glockenspiel) than a piano. It was dreamy and cool and, when amplified and effects applied, it was glorious. Along with the addition of a Fender electric bass, the sound of the Fender-Rhodes piano really catalysed Miles Davis's movement to his 'electric' period.

By the time Chick Corea added a ring modulator and echoplex tape delay to his setup in 1970, his Fender-Rhodes was completely transforming the trumpeter's compositions. Keith Jarrett entered the ensemble about this time, playing either an RMI electric piano or a Fender Contempo organ. It took Corea a while to come to grips with the instrument, saying that he 'struggled with it for a while, because I really didn't like it', but then began to 'see how to work it, and bring it more into the sonic thing that Miles was looking for'.[28]

The album *Live at Fillmore* and the group's filmed performance at the 1970 Isle of Wight Festival are good examples of the very complex electronic textures underpinning

Miles's music. Quartal parallelism, atonal riffs and patchwork of electronically produced sounds were circulating around the harmonically static, straight eight-note groove. Rather than thinking of this as the influence of rock music, it seems that the timbre and sustained lines and chords provided something that was much more forward-looking, about a stretching out of musical time, allowing the electronic and acoustic sounds to simply *be*. Ultimately, the aesthetic of this period of Davis's is much more akin to electronic music than rock: the recordings from this era, *In a Silent Way*, *Bitches Brew*, *Live at Fillmore*, *Live-evil* and *On the Corner*, are masterpieces that adumbrated the pulse-based neo-tonal ECM genre, techno, drum and bass and ambient music.

Feedback

It could be said that electronic music – literally and figuratively – is all about feedback. From the 'tail-chasing'[29] self-generating patches of analogue synthesis to the howling guitar of Jimi Hendrix, to the continual recycling and re-purposing of electronic equipment, it could be schematized as electronic and cultural feedback loops.

In 1906 Lee De Forest added a third filament to his vacuum tube (valve). What we now call the triode tube, De Forest dubbed the Audion. Six years later, an undergraduate student at Columbia University, experimenting with ways to increase the amplification of De Forest's Audion, discovered that sending some of the output signal back into the tubes input stage increased the overall gain of the triode. When one of De Forest's assistants accidentally fed the output signal of an Audion back on itself, the Audion would 'howl or sing'.[30]

The trick here, as experimenters and scientists soon found, was that the gain of the triode could be increased, but the loop had to be attenuated so the system did not begin to self-oscillate, or 'feed back' upon itself. In 1940 Harald Bode, who would go on to design a ring modulator and a pitch-shifter for Robert Moog twenty years later, had already understood the potentiality of the feedback loop:

> The engineer who embarks upon the design of a feedback amplifier must be a creature of mixed emotions. On the one hand, he can rejoice in the improvements in the characteristics of the structure which feedback promises to secure him. On the other hand, he knows that unless he can finally adjust the phase and attenuation characteristics around the feed-back loop so the amplifier will not spontaneously burst into uncontrollable singing none of the advantages can actually be realized.[31]

Feedback as an acoustical phenomenon is an obvious disruption. It occurs when an audio input, commonly a microphone or guitar pickup, and its amplified output – usually a loudspeaker – are situated in such a way that the amplified signal from the speaker is picked up again and again by the input stage. Initially this was as a nuisance in sound reinforcement and recording, but the sonic possibilities began to reveal themselves to musicians.

There are so many brilliant feedback stories. John Lennon claimed that the first use of feedback on a rock record was on the Beatles' 'I Feel Fine', saying 'I defy anybody to find a record . . . that uses feedback that way.'[32] During the session, Lennon had leaned his Gibson J-160e, an acoustic guitar with a built-in P-90 pickup, against his amplifier:

> John had just leaned it against the amp when it went 'Nnnnnnnwahhhhh.' And we went, 'What's that? Voodoo!'

'No, it's feedback' . . . George Martin was there so we said 'Can we have that on the record?' 'Well, I suppose we could, we could edit it on the front.' It was a found object.[33]

Charlie Butten, an electronics wizard who was working in a music store in San Francisco in 1967, got to know Cream's Eric Clapton when he converted their Marshall amps over to u.s. power for their Fillmore performances. He wasn't really prepared for how loud the group was, but gradually came around to their highly improvised music. By chance, he met up with Cream in New York a few months later:

Jim Marshall, at the time he built the amplifiers had no notion that they were going to be used this way. He had sort of pictured more like a Chet Atkins-type trip. At one point, he [Marshall] said to Eric: 'How do you use it?' And Eric said: 'I just turn everything [all the knobs, volume and tone controls] all the way up.' Marshall was absolutely astounded by this.[34]

Watching Cream perform, Butten realized that Clapton liked to use feedback in his playing. He was surprised to see the road crew propping up Clapton's Marshall stack from behind when he pressed against it to initiate feedback. Butten knew immediately that he could make things work much better. He took Clapton's Marshall apart and added a preamplifier stage to the amp, using an unused 'side' of one of the 12AX7 preamp tubes. He wired it to one of the input jacks on the amp, and painted it red. Butten said to Clapton: 'When you want feedback . . . plug into the red jack.'[35] Clapton was thrilled with this modification to his amplifier, and when Cream returned to England, he asked Jim Marshall to build him another one just like it.

Created only with guitars, amplifiers and a few outboard effects, Lou Reed's 1975 album *Metal Machine Music* is a tour de force of meta-guitar feedback and processing. Much maligned by rock audiences, Reed subtitled the four-movement record *An Electronic Instrumental Composition* and it represents a major departure from the use of feedback by many of rock's master guitarists. Here the guitar, *qua* guitar, is submerged – only a generator of feedback events, and hardly recognizable as a guitar at all.

The album was recorded in Reed's apartment using three tape recorders, five Marshall tube amplifiers, a ring modulator, tremolo units and reverberation units. During his time with the Velvet Underground, the musicians would often lean their guitars against their amps and walk away, letting them play themselves. He recollected:

> I would record tracks of guitar, at different speeds, playing with the reverb, tuning the guitars in unusual ways . . . I would tune all the strings, say, to E, put the guitar a certain distance from the amp, and it would start feeding back. The harmonics would start mixing, going into something else. It was as if the guitar was hitting itself.[36]

The music is monolithic and immersive, with high-register circular melodic fragments within layers of droning feedback. Reed pays homage to La Monte Young's The Theatre of Eternal Music on the album cover. John Cale, a member of the Velvets, was also a member of Young's ensemble. At Reed's instruction, mastering engineer Bob Ludwig placed a 'locked groove' at the end of the fourth movement. Thus the final seconds of the track would repeat ad infinitum until the tone arm was manually lifted. The album really was, as Reed titled it, electronic music, but it was released to rock audiences. In fact, *Metal Machine Music* turned out to be an important precursor to industrial music.

Reed's recording, sonically ahead of its time, was roundly criticized by conventional listeners. His record company withdrew it from the market only three weeks after its release. Despite this commercial misstep, it sold 100,000 copies and became a cult classic over the years. Rock critic Lester Bangs heard it as the revelatory music that is really was. He understood that *Metal Machine Music* was 'Lou's soul. If there is one thing he would like to see buried in a time capsule, this is it.'[37]

Circuits make sound immediately available to us – if we are so inclined – whether it might be creating a feedback loop, arranging a particular arrangement of guitar effects pedals, or even intervening in the circuitry itself with a soldering iron. They have given us a new knowledge of, and a new conceptual frame for, sound. They are the very building blocks of sound. Because circuits can be arranged in almost infinite configurations, they link the engineer, composer and performer in whole new ways. Circuits have created a new culture of sonic literacy by opening a rich and still-evolving connection between music and electronics. Circuits have surpassed, or at least provided an alternative to, traditional musical instruments and their established performance praxes and accepted musical genres. Circuits have made sound *ours* to shape and, most importantly, they have allowed us to create *our music*, forging new musical genres and new musical collectivities.

Afrika Bambaataa at the decks, c. 1980.

3
TURNTABLE AND RECORD

Some ten years before Schaeffer and Henry manipulated disc recordings in their Paris studio, John Cage had begun to see the possibilities of the turntable and records as instruments. He was working at Seattle's Cornish College of the Arts as a dance accompanist in the autumn of 1938, and with his unique ability to recognize fresh and unlikely musical relationships, juxtaposed available traditional instruments and sound equipment within the same temporal frame:

> I was attracted there in the first place by the presence of a large collection of percussion instruments; but when I got there I discovered that there was a radio station in connection with the school . . . and we were able to make experiments combining percussion instruments and small sounds that required amplification in the studio. We were able to broadcast those to the theater which was just a few steps away, and we were able, of course, to make recordings and, besides making records, to use records as instruments.[1]

Cage, delighted with this improvised arrangement of percussion and sound technology, composed his famous 1939 composition *Imaginary Landscape No. 1*, scored for four performers using two turntables playing RCA Victor test records, gong and piano. Much later, Cage described his discoveries:

> When you change the speed of the record, you change the frequency of the recorded sound. I used continuous sounds that were made for test purposes by the Victor Company, and they had both constant tones and tones that were constantly sliding in pitch through a whole range.[2]

While Cage developed the pitch-change possibilities of the variable speed turntable in *Imaginary Landscape No. 1*, Pierre Schaeffer saw the timbral changes inherent in this process while composing his *Railway Study*:

> I have obtained some quite remarkable transformations by playing a fragment recorded at 78 rpm at 33 rpm. By playing the record at rather less than half speed, everything goes down a bit more than an octave and the tempo slows at the same rate. With this apparently quantitative change there is also a qualitative phenomenon. The 'railway' element at half speed isn't the slightest bit like a railway. It turns into a foundry and a blast furnace.[3]

Schaeffer would go on to call this 'qualitative phenomenon' anamorphosis, the variable, non-linear associations between transformations of a physical audio signal and their auditory perceptions. Schaeffer borrowed the concept from art history, where anamorphosis refers to a distorted projection or drawing that appears normal when viewed from a particular angle or with some kind of mirror or lens. The most famous example of anamorphosis in painting is *The Ambassadors* (1533) by Hans Holbein the Younger. In the bottom centre of the canvas is an anamorphic skull.

Although Cage, Schaeffer and Henry broke into the technology of the turntable to repurpose and musically activate it, the deeper possibilities of the turntable as an instrument remained submerged until 1970 when Clive Campbell, a Jamaican-born disc jockey known as DJ Kool Herc, began to develop breakbeat techniques that allowed him to create a continuous 'new' music. This technique, requiring two turntables and a stereo mixer, was transformative in a number of ways:

> I was listening to American music in Jamaica and my favorite artist was James Brown. That's who inspired me. A lot of the records I played were by James Brown . . . So what I did here was go right to the 'yoke.' I cut off all anticipation and played the beats. I'd find out where the break in the record was at and prolong it and people would love it.[4]

Jamaica holds pride of place in the history of international DJ culture. Their 'sound systems' are the collective name of teams of DJs, sound people and MCs who play ska, rocksteady or reggae. Beginning in Kingston in the 1950s, a truck, a portable petrol generator and sound equipment made a portable set-up for giving street parties. Each 'sound system' developed its own identity and fan base. This musical practice was critical in fostering the Jamaican musical genres that eventually became wildly popular internationally.

It was also in Jamaica that DJs developed the completely original and brilliant practice of 'dubplating'. The dubplate is a singular pressing on an acetate disc that contains unreleased music or remixes. Record companies used them regularly as test discs, simply a way to make certain that everything was in order before an expensive and time-consuming vinyl production run. They were less expensive to produce than the mass-produced vinyl record, though they wore out quickly. Wearing out quickly was, in this case, a positive outcome. As a contemporary DJ explained:

> It was the cheapest and best way of being able to play a new song on a soundsystem or in a club. So back in the day you had two choices: you could come with a cassette or you had the dubplate. It's a way of testing out a song, but the Jamaican soundsystem clash culture started using it for more exclusive public performances for a one-off song that no one else has got.[5]

This practice is fascinating conceptually because a dubplate becomes a unique musical object, desirable precisely because its musical effects are ephemeral and performative. In terms of production, this is a complete reversal of the usual chain of product creation and consumption. The record was originally a vehicle carrying repetition, but the 'off-market' dubplate performance gave you what 'no one else has got'. You had to be there.

New Tools and Techniques

Since its release in 1978 the Technics SL-1200MK2 and its subsequent versions have been by far the most common turntable for DJing. Producers, DJs and MCs refer to the Technics turntable as the 'Tec 12's', 'Wheels of Steel' and 'Ones & Twos'. It featured a 'direct-drive' motor (no belt) and a start/stop push button, and it was capable of reaching its playing speed quickly. There was also a pitch control which aided the DJ when matching beats between a pair of turntables. Add to this the usual Vestax crossfader, amplifier and speakers, and you have made a new musical instrument.

The sonic and artistic impact of the repurposed turntable is inestimable. In the short term, a whole new musical genre of rap/hip-hop flourished as Afrika Bambaataa, and Grandmaster Flash, and Grand Wizard Theodore quickly developed a virtuosic performance practice *manually* manipulating turntables in live performance. Effectively, all of the 'tape techniques' of *musique concrète* – the cut, the edit, speed change, tape reversal and their accompanying anamorphic potential – became possible in this new performance practice.

These turntable techniques acquired their own names such as breaks, needle-drop, crab scratch and beat juggling. Miles White, undertaking an organological study, writes that

> a number of modifications had been made to the phonograph, the most critical of which involves the addition of a peripheral unit called an audio-mixer . . . The audio mixer has an on-board cross-fader component, a horizontal sliding lever which allows the performer to effect certain techniques on a single disc or to move easily back and forth between two turntables when working with multiple discs.[6]

He goes on to codify the following performance techniques: for the single turntable they are 'backspinning, scratching, and cutting'; for dual turntables they are 'mixing, blending, and punch-phrasing'.[7]

Backspinning (or backcueing) is the manipulation of the phonograph disc back and forth on the turntable platter. It can be used to cue record fragments and create manual sound loops or the iconic 'scratch' where a sound fragment can be rhythmicized. Cutting is a macrosound technique involving 'the reconfiguration of a textual or musical segment using repetition and selective editing'.[8] Using two turntables allows the use of two or more recordings. While one record is playing, the DJ can cue another disc and even 'beat match' it using headphones, before using the crossfader to bring it into the audience mix.

One of the most common techniques is Kool Herc's, using two identical records, isolating a breakbeat and alternating between the two turntables by backspinning and crossfading to keep the beat going indefinitely.

Hip-hop turntable techniques found their way into multiple genres. Turntablism, as it is now commonly called, is a two-part counter-consumption procedure. First, the turntable is played like a traditional musical instrument, something its inventors never intended. Secondly, the record itself is now a 'random access' form of analogue musical history.

David Albert Mhadi Goldberg, a DJ and scholar of rap music, understands the very sophisticated effects of these techniques and their musical significance. He describes the early hip-hop experiments as 'scratched deconstruction', that is,

> the theoretical and manual exploration of a recording's composition in terms of its pitch, tone, timing, content, and meaning. The scratch can subdivide a sound along its internal boundaries and rearrange its units, forming entirely new aural moments. Scratching the recorded voice or other discrete sound moves it from word, syllable, or phoneme to hand-driven sonic turbulence that can take on the character-istics of drumlike percussion, stringlike friction, and windlike pitch shifts.[9]

These techniques, then, brought to the fore the often subtle but perceptually critical 'structural' noise within sound (for example, the noisy attack transients of the beginnings of many instrumental and vocal sounds), relocating it on the musical surface.

If tape recording and its associated manipulations removed sounds from their sources and offered new organizational strategies, turntable techniques interrupted the homogeneity of mass-produced musical commodities even more forcefully and allowed for the noise of social relations hidden by standardized music production, which effectively removed traces of difference.

The philosopher Richard Shusterman, working from the lexicon of cultural studies and postmodernism, describes these hip-hop practices as 'appropriative sampling':

> appropriation rather than unique originative creation, the eclectic mixing of styles, the enthusiastic embracing of the new technology and mass culture, the challenging of modernist notions of aesthetic autonomy and artistic purity, and an emphasis on the localized and temporal rather than the putatively universal and eternal.[10]

Significantly, both dub reggae DJs and hip-hop artists participate in the same global aesthetics and economics that govern the postmodern as it is commonly understood, but as Shusterman strongly implies, this appropriation of technologies and materials should be understood as local. Much of the innovation in electronic music I am describing in dub and hip-hop was situated initially in very different cultural and geographic domains than those inhabited by the more privileged heirs of modernism. Theoretically, their contributions are a form of appropriation, but the performances and techniques of these early dub and hip-hop artists might also be described as a kind of material gleaning – picking up and reusing the materials that planned scarcity and surplus have materially and culturally discarded.

Although hip-hop has inevitably been re-commodified (as Jacques Attali insists, 'where there is music, there is money'[11]), its cultural roots were not in dominant musical culture. Furthermore, the musical innovations we are describing are not limited to production by professionals or amateurs, but included a huge shift in the technology of listening by new consumers.

In scope, imagination and technique nothing matched 'The Adventures of Grandmaster Flash on the Wheels of Steel', a single released by Grandmaster Flash in 1981. It is hard to even imagine the energy of this live DJ performance of Flash scratching and mixing an astonishing range of records using three turntables, the 'wheels of steel'. Flash, himself, notes, with no undue modesty, that it is

> The first record ever that's a DJ solo. No house band. No rappers . . . just me, my gear, my beats, and my techniques . . . I finally got my own record. Finally got to punch-phase, cue, cut, spin back, rub, and zuka-zuka on wax.[12]

Done in just four takes in the studio, the piece was constructed with a moment of the soundtrack of the film *Flash Gordon* and Jackson Beck's 'The Decoys of Ming the Merciless', Blondie's 'Rapture', Chic's 'Good Times', The Furious Five's 'Birthday Party', The Hellers' 'Life Story', Queen's 'Another One Bites the Dust', Spoonie Gee's 'Monster Jam', The Sugarhill Gang's '8th Wonder' and 'Rapper's Delight', The Incredible Bongo Band's 'Apache', and Flash's own earlier recording 'Freedom'.

In addition to the stunning virtuosity of the turntable techniques in 'The Adventures of Grandmaster Flash on the Wheels of Steel', the recording suggests a new kind of musical history – with the record collection as a random-access archive of music that could be freely taken up and dissected, reassembled and recomposed in the most playful ways.

Near the middle of Flash's eight-minute piece, we hear children's voices saying 'please tell me a story.' A man's voice then says, 'I think I'll tell you the story of my life.' After saying where he was born, he then says, 'and now I'm lucky enough to be here with you.' This intercut 'story', jumping from birth into the flow of the present, models a new kind of narrative that 'record cutting' could provide: the sound recording no longer as a repository of sounds in a fixed order, but in a constant state of 'becoming'. Like the jump cut in film editing, it provides the listener with the possibility of unexpected juxtapositions, and a sense of time dislocated.

There is, of course, a long history of borrowing and quotation in Western classical music. Early forms of Western polyphonic music were based on existing chant melodies. Some of these appropriations were deliberately transgressive. Late Renaissance composers, for instance, incorporated secular and even bawdy melodies banned by the Church into their sacred compositions.

I would insist, however, that more contemporary appropriation, facilitated at the most basic level of sound, was unprecedented. As it was creatively misused by these practitioners, it represented in its inception a kind of necessary, rough and physical intervention into the conservative logic of the commercial record industry. It was bold, furiously creative and musically utopian. Had it not been for the legal intervention of the record industry, this amazing intertextual compositional practice might have flourished above ground.

The brave work of the Canadian artist John Corbett, who believes that this kind of work falls under the tenets of 'fair use', is probably the best example of musical civil disobedience. His 'plunderphonics', remixes and cut-ups of famous pieces by people such as Dolly Parton and Michael Jackson, drew threats of litigation, causing Corbett to remove his work from general circulation.[13]

As it is, this practice continues, but what were once the surface features of joyous, democratic, inclusive, genre-busting musical borrowing have been relegated to the sonic underground.

In the Grooves

In 1985 Christian Marclay released *Record Without a Cover*, a twelve-inch vinyl LP. Pressed into the vinyl on one side of the LP is the directive 'DO NOT STORE IN A PROTECTIVE PACKAGE.' The record, with a single track that contained various glitches, musical samples and sections of silence, was intended to become a personalized object for each listener as it began to gather its own dust particles, scratches, dirt and fingerprints. Quickly becoming a collector's item, Marclay's highly conceptual record certainly calls into question the idea of a recording as a monadic, mechanically reproducible work of art. It also involves the owner as collaborator in a continually evolving 'composition'.

Marclay's brilliant interventions during these years constituted direct interventions in the material components of records, right into the record grooves themselves. Perhaps his 1981 composition *One Thousand Cycles* is the best indication of this. Marclay made what he termed 'recycled' records:

> These records are collages I made by cutting vinyl records into pieces and reconfiguring them into different combinations. The rhythmic pops are the actual cuts between the different shards of vinyl.[14]

In *Groove* (1982), Marclay created an eight-track texture using multiple passes of the same seven-inch single. He notes that he 'created the loops by sticking little dot stickers directly on the vinyl, which caused the needle to skip'.[15] His use of records with off-centre holes is another example of altering the material design of the vinyl medium, resulting in 'frequency modulation' of the music stored there.

Marclay also took the turntable mechanism itself to logical extremes. One technique is the arrangement of two side-by-side turntables and sharing their two-tone arms on just one of the records. This technique produced various tape loop effects. His 1985 piece *Ghost (I Don't Live Today)* uses a turntable worn like a guitar. The sound material is The Jimi Hendrix Experience's record 'I Don't Live Today', subjected to unorthodox, noisy techniques on the repurposed device.

Though trained as a visual artist, the English sound artist Philip Jeck has worked with turntables since the early 1980s. Jeck is well known for his 1993 audio installation, *Vinyl Requiem*, which used as many as 180 turntables. With the addition of tape recorders and other vintage electronics, he has produced remarkable works on lo-fi turntables with records as 'found' sound objects. The sound of old vinyl records – their scratches, dust and band-limited timbres – gives his music a sense of haunting, slowly repeating sonic dreams characterized by bits of music, deliberately looped moments and fragments of speech. Jeck refers to his collection of records as 'memory packages':

> They do sort of carry their history with them, which is part of the attraction. When you think about the amount of information that can gather on them, especially compared to recorded sound now, they really are little memory discs. Each one of them has so many different things stored in their grooves. In quite a crude way, they have history on them because of the scratches and the damage and the warping that has occurred over time ... and even if you don't recognise the actual original record, there will be some sounds in there that will conjure

up some memory or feeling from some time. I do feel like
I'm playing with memory and history when I'm playing these
records.[16]

His 2000 recording *Vinyl Coda I–III* comprises three long
live performances that are quietly virtuosic. Regarding the sonic
qualities of his music, Jeck states:

The record players that I'm using are old – they're not high
fidelity and their speed is not that regular – they already
change or distort the sound, so immediately they bring their
colour to it . . . You put the needle to the record and that's the
sound. You put your hand on the record and it slows the sound
down; you see how the thing works and you can understand
what the function is . . . So I really like that about these old
record players. It's all really tactile and I really like the way
I can manipulate the sound directly.[17]

How has all this changed how we think about music? As a
particular form of remembering in the literal sense – of putting
back together pieces – it opens up new possible meanings.
Musical time, musical history and musical moments, phrases,
even the glitch of surface noise on a record, have become
new sound objects, infinitely accessible, remixable and
re-composable by professionals and savvy amateurs.

The emphasis on 'turntablism' as a new technique of
production may have left out someone and something: what
has happened to the mindful listener and where is the record
itself that, after all, still contains the sonic materials and
musical possibilities we have described? Towards an answer to
these remaining questions, let me offer a kind of personal and
theoretical coda.

Towards a Sonic Materialism: When a Record is a Thing (of Beauty)

My point of departure is a rather subjective experience, but one that may be familiar or, at least, recognized sufficiently to lead to an interesting and valid question in relation to music and sonic culture. I am referring to the sense of disappointment I have often felt while attending a live performance of music that I have come to admire as a recording. Much attention has been given, of course, to the opposing formulation that it is the recording that falls short, and to the assumption that the experience of listening to the recording can only be an inadequate substitute for hearing the 'real' thing live and in performance. Walter Benjamin's famous 1936 essay, 'The Work of Art in the Age of Mechanical Reproduction', is the most emphatic statement of a certain sense of loss of power and beauty around what he refers to as 'aura'. I will describe with a few examples what I'm referring to as a 'disappointment', moving in a reverse sequence from record to live performance.

When I was fourteen years old, I went to see The Jimi Hendrix Experience in concert. Six months before, I had bought the album *Are You Experienced?*, shortly after hearing Hendrix's hit single 'Purple Haze' on the radio in my Midwestern city. I listened to the album constantly. It was a kind of musical lifeline. I was very excited to hear Hendrix and his trio in concert. I remember quite a bit visually about the concert – it was a spectacle, with Hendrix smashing up his guitar at the end, but my sonic recollections are that it was very loud and musically sloppy. The tempos were 'too fast', the vocal performances rather indifferent; this was my first real disappointment at a live performance. I might add that in the intervening years, I have occasionally listened to bootlegged live recordings of Jimi Hendrix (usually recorded off of the live sound board), and these confirmed my experience.

At the age of 32, Glenn Gould played his final public concert on Friday, 10 April 1964, at the Wilshire Ebell Theatre in Los Angeles, California. He played four fugues from Bach's *The Art of Fugue*, Bach's Partita No. 4 in D major, Beethoven's Sonata Op. 109 and Hindemith's Sonata No. 3.

After that, Gould scandalized the classical music world by giving up live performance altogether, declaring, 'The concert is dead.' The pianist stated that live concerts were demeaning, and that he 'detested audiences'. Ultimately, Gould's radical decision to only make recordings in the future was further compounded as we learned that he had begun to embrace the recording medium as fully as many rock musicians had done.

In his 1966 article 'The Prospects of Recording', Gould's criticism of the romanticization and spectacularization of the artist at the expense of appreciating the artwork had many implications. He writes: 'the determination of the value of the work of art according to the information available about it is a most delinquent form of aesthetic appraisal.'[18] Gould is referring here to the tape splice, and ends up justifying it by effectively saying: Yes, I spliced up this Bach fugue because it made for a more musical rendering than I could have done live, and only after reflection on the recorded objects. But most importantly I think he is suggesting that the listener to his recording would be unaware that it was made from two takes, unless Gould himself had revealed it.

Within the world of classical music, tape splicing was sacrilegious – up to that point, the recording medium was thought of only as a stand-in for a concert performance. The issue here was that, for Gould, live performance no longer laid claim to the optimal appreciation of classical music. What's more, he had begun to see the recording studio as a meta-compositional tool.

In his article, Gould had used the examples of blown art and musical forgeries to argue for the validity of post-production techniques, in particular the tape splice. Ten years later, Gould elaborated further on live performance versus recording when he wrote about discovering equalization:

> From the moment I began broadcasting, that medium seemed like another world, as indeed it is. The moment I began to experience the studio environment, my whole reaction to what I could do with music under the proper circumstances changed totally. From then on, concerts were less than second best – they were merely something to be gotten through. They were a very poor substitute for a real artistic experience . . . My first nationwide network broadcast was in 1950, when I was seventeen. I remember, among other things, playing the Mozart Sonata, K. 281. The studio piano actually had a rather nice sound, but a rotten action and a very thick bass; and I was very depressed about the result, because I knew what I wanted from that sonata, and I wasn't able to get it on that instrument. However, I took an acetate home the same day, put it on the turntable, and began to fiddle with the treble-bass control, which, of course, was very primitive in those days. Nevertheless, I was able to minimize that thick bass by emphasizing the upper frequencies, and so that piano became electronically altered after the fact, if you will. It now had an altogether more appealing sound than that which I was able to achieve under 'real, live' conditions.[19]

Rock writer Michael Lydon describes a similar experience in his chapter 'Are Records Music?' in his 1974 book *Boogie Lightning*.[20] He learns that his beloved Buck Clayton record of a single-take jazz jam was actually 'stitched together from two versions done in the studio'. He writes: 'That news was mildly upsetting, but it did not diminish my digging the record because I couldn't hear the difference.'[21]

Lydon goes on to point out that after all, recording is as artificial as film-making, yet records, like film, have the strangely convincing reality of technologically perfect reproduction.[22] Later writers have mentioned this connection with film, that its iterability and fixedness are rarely criticized as alienating, and the issue of 'original versus copy' is rarely thought to be problematic. Gould invokes the same argument in 'The Prospects of Recording'.

Lydon goes even further to say (about the grooves of a record) that 'those wiggles are the music'. This assertion, in addition to the one that the record is a kind of 'plastic sculpture',[23] gives us an unexpected snapshot of the record as a thing (of beauty), but I have in mind another angle. To elaborate, let us consider briefly the recording process itself as leading to a different sort of materiality.

The Grain of the Record

In his famous essay 'The Grain of the Voice', Roland Barthes describes 'grain' as a bodily intersection of language and the singing voice.[24] As much as I admire his formulation, I am invoking 'grain' in this context as a woodworker might, where every planed board reveals an individual pattern of light and dark wood resulting from varying growth conditions. I would say that every recording has a grain, and the most important contributor to the grain is what is known as 'room tone'. Room tone is largely the sound of the particular silence of a space. I say 'particular silence', because there is no such thing as a truly silent room except an anechoic chamber, a room designed to completely absorb sound reflections. The anechoic chamber must also be completely isolated from exterior sound and structure-born sound: no easy task. Room tone is an extremely complex entity that is a completely variable mix of room resonance that is created by standing waves, reverberation time, the absorption coefficient of the walls, floors, furniture, people and instruments, and finally simply whatever ambient sound is present there.

Standing waves are a primary factor in creating room tone. Standing waves in rooms can cause certain resonant frequencies to either be boosted in amplitude (called 'nodes') or cancelled out altogether (called 'antinodes'). The nodes have longer reverberation times and we perceive those nodal frequencies as louder. So the bottom line is that rooms effectively produce *tones*, because there is always sound present in them – again, they are never truly silent.

Alvin Lucier's *I am Sitting in a Room* is a classic electronic process piece that takes advantage of room standing waves to slowly and gradually submerge the composer's recorded speech act into a set of continuously resonating room tones. As the composer's speech is played back and recorded over and over again in the same space, the room effectively begins to harmonize itself as the standing waves gradually increase in volume, while the speech itself fades out.

Placing a microphone in the space is the next term of this sonic equation. Every location will have a distinct *presence* created by the position of the microphone in relation to its spatial boundaries and all of the factors previously mentioned. A microphone placed in two different locations of the same room can produce two very different presences. Using more than one microphone then increases the number of possible presences exponentially. I want to comment on the word 'presence' here. Whereas room tone is what an acoustician or recording engineer would call it, a casual listener will often use the word 'presence' or even speak of a space's 'intimacy'. Room tone or presence or intimacy present on a record is a key part of how the listener 'learns' a record.

Next, we would have to add that the type (dynamic, condenser, tube condenser or ribbon) and even make of microphone will greatly influence the room tone, as will the placement of instruments and the musicians themselves. Add then, the signal path of the microphones, the audio console, any outboard equipment such as a compressor, an equalizer and so on, and we are left with a huge set of electroacoustic variables.

At some recording sessions, the engineer will set everything up and record a minute or so of room tone to allow for greater flexibility in the post-production phase. If one was to splice in analogue leader tape or, nowadays, 'digital black', the result would be quite jarring, even though it's supposed to be silence.

The recording process also provides a more or less built-in feature that can improve listening conditions remarkably. Recordings *compress* the signals recorded. That is to say, recordings have a smaller dynamic range compared to the ear. The recording compresses the dynamic range by some forty decibels. What does this mean? The aural result is that the perceived 'distance' between the loudest sounds and the quietest sounds on a recording is smaller. Thus the listener simply more easily apprehends a recording's presence and its flow of electroacoustic objects.

The Chain of Sonic Custody

Taken as a whole, it is these qualities of the record that provide a sonic continuity often lost or contaminated in the live performance. Another anecdote: I acquired Bruno Walter's 1957 recording of Gustav Mahler's Symphony No. 9, released by Columbia Records on its short-lived 'budget' Odyssey series, because I liked the cover and it was cheap. This recording was made with the Columbia Symphony Orchestra, a pick-up ensemble drawn from leading New York musicians. It is a magical musical performance that I have gone back to again and again.

In later years, I strove in vain to experience a live performance of this composition that didn't disappoint me. I might add that just a few months ago, I was discussing Mahler's Symphony No. 9 with a close composer friend. I mentioned the Walter recording in question, and before I could even finish my sentence, he blurted out that for him this record *was* the piece. I could scarcely believe my ears. We then discussed what amounted to the 'aura' of this record, the warmth and presence of the strings, the balance of the brass and the Zen of Mahler that Walter (and producer John McClure) had created for us. I say us, because here were two people who never knew each other at the time we first owned the recording, and lived a thousand miles apart, yet had a similar experience. What this experience opened up for me is the relationship between the original and replicates, oneness versus multiplicity, and the individual and the group. We all understand that the concert is a communal opportunity, but there *is* a comparable sociality associated with the record.

It seems to me that, thanks to the work of art in the age of mechanical reproduction, my friend and I were hearing the same flow of electroacoustic objects, the same ones each time we relistened to the piece, so that we could have switched records and still had a similar experience. So, it seems that mechanical reproduction does contain the possibility then for a positive communal experience, rather than the distracting, alienating one Benjamin theorized.

Sound touches us. It touches us all the time, and recorded sound touches us no more or less than live sound. The sound of a record is as tactile and embodied as a live performance, but the electroacoustic sound objects that records generate are optimally organized to provide a highly coherent listening experience with regard to such things as dynamic range, frequency response and stereo image.

Theorist John Durham Peters reminds us that as far back as the nineteenth century, physicist Hermann von Helmholtz understood the ear 'levels all modalities'.[25] In fact, the mechanism of the ear is much like a musical instrument that, when receiving a stimulus, (re)creates sound – a 'piano in the ear', as Peters describes it.[26]

This 'levelling' capacity of the ear, along with higher-fidelity recording and reproduction technology, played a primary role in creating new modalities of record listening after the 1950s. In a very real sense, better sound (re)production has allowed the ear to do its job to the very fullest extent. For example, listening to music on an excellent pair of headphones can do much to make the physical connection of recorded sound to the ear far more efficient. Headphones allow the listener to hear new levels of detail that might not have been possible otherwise. The amazing capacity of the human ear to process sound has been enhanced through new technology and listening practices.

The final link in the chain of sonic custody is the built space. Record listening radically transforms the architectural space we inhabit. It makes sense that better recording and listening technology would begin to allow us to more fully animate the spaces in which we listen. Thus the last link in the 'chain of sonic custody' is the listener's relationship to architectural space. As architectural theorist Björn Hellström writes: 'This process is a multi-dimensional tool and simultaneously and continuously it operates between an active/ passive, determined/undetermined order by decoding sonic information: we "create" the surrounding space by our listening apparatus.'[27] Nowadays, contemporary electronic musicians and sound/installation artists are engaged in a more symbiotic transformation of space and subjectivity. Lydon argues that

> Those of us who came to musical consciousness in the 1950s accept records as music . . . Little Richard's 'Ready Teddy' is still a musical experience for me the thousandth time around . . . Since I believe my experiences are real, I believe records are music.[28]

To say that 'records are music' seems a simple proposition to the attentive listener. Additionally, the phonograph record reshaped the DJ as composer, teacher and archivist. In its most profound effects, the phonograph record itself must now be understood as a material sonic apparatus, a complete musical 'thing' comparable to any other instrumental advance in electronic music.

Laurie Anderson, performance artist, crouching by a white violin and a microphone stand, mid-1980s.

4

MICROPHONE

In 1990 the Society for Ethnomusicology published a
report entitled *Demystifying and Classifying Electronic Music
Instruments*. On the face of it, the project was encouraging to
electronic musicians because it situated their work as part of
'the ongoing process of developments in musics of the world'.
This capacious definition of music made room for many new
instruments:

> the 'scratch turntable' used in rap music would best be classi-
> fied as an electric scraped idiophone [an instrument the whole
> of which vibrates to produce a sound when struck, shaken,
> or scraped] . . . On a more esoteric note, another problematic
> example is the use of a cactus plant from which the needles
> are extracted. The sound of needles being pulled from the
> plant is amplified. John Cage has used this in his composition
> *Child of Tree* (1975). We suggest that this could be classified
> either as a plucked idiophone . . . or as an amplified plosive
> aerophone [an instrument that produces sound primarily by
> causing a body of air to vibrate].[1]

Remarkably, the microphone appeared nowhere in this
exhaustive classification. Given their claims to inclusivity,

this was quite an oversight. Like so many technological advances, the advent of the microphone brought with it many misunderstandings and underestimations of its potential. Still, many practising musicians understood its complexities.

Since the 1920s, beginning with the 'microphone singers' like Bing Crosby – who may not have had a career without it – the microphone has been increasingly understood as an instrument. Frank Sinatra convincingly argued that the microphone was the modern singer's instrument, requiring the same level of practice and respect required by any traditional acoustic instrument:

> One thing that was tremendously important [to me] was learning the use of the microphone. Many singers never learned to use one. They never understood, and still don't, that a microphone is their instrument.[2]

Amplification of the voice is probably the most common association with the microphone. Its political as well as cultural significance as an instrument of vocal persuasion and dominance was often noted by twentieth-century historians and critics.

The microphone, however, did not merely amplify the human voice. Much more significantly, it freed the vocal utterance from its physical and psychoacoustic bounds. Any sound, in fact, amplified sufficiently could make audible what otherwise would be inaudible. The microphone effectively overrides the proximal limitations of even the quietest sounds – the sounds of the ambient world that we normally ignore. In this sense, the microphone acts as an extension not only of the human voice, but of the ear, reconfiguring the listener.

In one of the most interesting meditations on the psychoacoustics of the microphone, Ian Penman describes the microphone as a kind of super-listener, a stand-in for the analyst's 'calm, promiscuous ear: neutral, forgiving, open to everything, the slightest trace or stammer or spoken mark'.[3] Penman's great insight is that, like the psychoanalyst, the microphone 'listens for things no one has noted before', that it 'produces new takes, new topologies, new topographies'.[4] It is striking how much more a microphone 'hears' than a human subject listening at the same time in the space. Run the tape back, and a whole multitude of previously unheard sound events will cluster in and around what 'you thought you heard'.[5]

Still, the microphone is not as open, neutral and forgiving as one might think. Rather, it is quite unique in its sonic nature, very much depending on the type of microphone it is, the components used to produce it, and the way it is deployed in acoustic space. These things lead the microphone to be used for specific purposes. Not all microphones are created equal – one microphone might be more useful than another in capturing a certain sound event.

Consider the microphone as an electro-mechanical ear. A very simplified explanation of human hearing will give a good sense of how and why a microphone works. When any sound source is set into vibration, the air around it is set into sympathetic vibration. This sympathetic vibration amounts to oscillations of air pressure, where the air molecules periodically undergo compression and rarefaction. Without the intervening medium of air, there would be no sound at all. When the air pressure variations reach the eardrum, it begins to move back and forth in the same pattern as the original sound emitter.

The eardrum converts the air pressure variations to mechanical oscillations. Three tiny bones to the inner ear, or cochlea, then transmit these mechanical oscillations. Here, the vibrations are sorted according to frequency ranges. Remarkably, receptor cells on the basilar membrane react only in a limited region whose position depends on the frequency of the pitch. The receptor cells then convert the vibration to nerve impulses. Finally, the auditory nervous system transmits the neural signals to the brain, where the information is processed.

What happens in the ear when two or more sounds or tones are present? As psychoacoustican Juan Roederer explains, the eardrum responds with a complex pattern of vibration that is the sum of all of the air pressure changes (sounds) that are within earshot:

> The eardrum 'does not know' and 'does not care' about the fact that this pattern is really the result of the sum of two others [or more]. It has just *one* vibration pattern, of varying amplitude . . . this rather complicated, but single, vibration pattern . . . gives rise to *two* [or more] resonance regions of the basilar membrane . . . This property of the cochlea to disentangle a complex vibration pattern into the original pure tone components is called *frequency discrimination*.[6]

So the microphone has a diaphragm that is just an 'eardrum'. It has no inner ear or brain to sort and process the sound (or sounds). Like the eardrum, it simply vibrates to a single, complex vibration pattern that is the sum of all the sounds with strong enough air pressure variations to be 'heard'. The diaphragm's mechanical movement is converted to a fluctuating voltage that, again, corresponds to the complex pattern of the air pressure variation. Record or amplify it, and the ear will pick up the reproduced sound and do the same thing it would if the sound were a completely acoustic event.

The history of the microphone begins in the mid-nineteenth century. A German physicist named Johann Reis constructed a 'sound transmitter' that involved a metal strip sitting on a membrane. It had a metal point contact that completed a varying electrical circuit. Its quality was quite poor. In 1876 Elisha Gray and Alexander Graham Bell both developed a 'liquid transmitter' in which the diaphragm was attached to two conductive rods connected to a battery within an acidic solution. Sound pressure variations caused the two rods to separate from each other, changing the current flowing through the circuit.

David Hughes and Thomas Edison continued work on the microphone using carbon granules. Here, the varying pressure of the diaphragm changed the electrical resistance through the pack of granules. The quality was still poor and inventors then experimented with quartz crystals.

E. C. Wente developed the condenser microphone in 1917 at Bell Labs. It was also known as a capacitor microphone or electrostatic microphone, and it converted sound waves into electrical waves that could be transmitted by the vacuum tube amplifier. In a condenser microphone, the diaphragm acts as one plate of a capacitor, and the vibrations produce changes in the distance between the plates. The invention of the vacuum tube (thermionic valve) was a key factor in pushing this technology forward. Condenser microphones were in use at the BBC starting around 1926, but were considered temperamental because moisture could cause 'frying noises' in them.[7]

Electromagnetic microphones, commonly known as 'dynamic' microphones (moving coil, moving iron and ribbon microphones) were later developments because early permanent magnets were very weak. It was only after the Second World War that stronger permanent magnets made this kind of design feasible. In this design, a small electrical transformer, positioned in the magnetic field of a permanent magnet, is connected to the diaphragm. A sound wave moves the diaphragm, which in turn causes the transformer to move in the magnetic field, creating an alternating current.

Early microphones were 'omni-directional', which is to say that they 'heard' in a 360-degree pattern. The ribbon microphone could detect sound in a bi-directional pattern (also called a figure-of-eight) because the ribbon is open on both sides. As microphone design advanced, more patterns became available. Nowadays, seven patterns are found, Omnidirectional, bi-directional or figure-of-eight, cardioid, sub-cardioid, hyper-cardioid, super-cardioid and a highly directional pattern known as a 'shotgun' pattern. Large diaphragm microphones are often used for picking up lower-frequency instruments like bass drums. Small condenser microphones often work well with sounds that have fast onset transients like cymbals and plucked strings. All are useful, but are to the recording engineer as different brushes are to a painter.

The difficulties of recording a large orchestra are multiple. With a large number of musicians playing many different kinds of instrument, the task is to both capture the individual sections of the orchestra (strings, brass, winds, percussion) and produce a sonically coherent whole, as a concert-goer would hear it. As the stereo format began to emerge in classical music recording, two engineers who worked for Decca records, Roy Wallace and Arthur Haddy, began experimenting with new ways to record in stereo, while still maintaining the recording's mono compatibility. At the time, record companies were releasing records in both mono and stereo formats for a number of years as the changeover to stereo took place. Roy Wallace thought that a three-microphone array might provide this compatibility and, at the same time, address the issue of recording a large number of instruments. He assembled a steel T-shaped bar and attached Neumann M49 microphones to each end, and a third in the centre. Reportedly, Haddy walked into the studio and declared: 'It looks like a bloody Christmas tree!'[8] The new device quickly became known as 'the Decca Tree'.

The microphone can be an uncontrollable beast or a comfortable, old friend. When faced with a microphone, the uninitiated speaker blows into it, holds it in the wrong place, speaks too softly or too loudly, or ignores it altogether. The late-night jazz DJ learned to use the 'proximity effect', a characteristic of the unidirectional microphone that produces an up-close, smooth, 'bassy' sound that envelops and bathes the listener in a vocal sound that feathers the edges around the music itself.

Because the microphone is so physically connected to sound waves, the actual perturbations in the air, it stands apart as a technological innovation. It is a particularly intimate and revealing technology. The microphone changed the way listeners understood what they heard, transforming what might be considered a kind of sonic unconscious into interpretable language. The combination of the microphone and recording media gave one the ability to listen repeatedly. This experience has allowed the listener to gain new levels of musical competence.

We might think of the microphone as another kind of interpreter of material in a way analogous to the human ear. It dictates individual perception of sound, not because it is so 'accurate', 'true' or capable of capturing sounds as they are, but rather because it admits relatively subjective avenues for capturing and distinguishing sound.

Composers are, above all, trained listeners. The very nature of the microphone would suggest that the device might, in some way, take the place of the composer's ear or circumvent the composer altogether. Arguably, using a microphone in this way would effectively relinquish the authority of the composer as the artistic mediator of sounds. On the other hand, the acoustical properties of the microphone, particularly its sensitivity to sound, mean that it could be turned towards sound-making rather than sound-collecting. This may be the reason why the microphone as a compositional tool is musically represented in a relatively small number of pieces. These compositions are, however, widely appreciated as unique and compelling.

Stockhausen: *Mikrophonie I*

Mikrophonie I (1964), the first composition to use the microphone as an instrument, was the indirect result of Karlheinz Stockhausen's purchase of a large tam-tam for his acoustic ensemble composition *Momente*, written in the early 1960s. The huge gong was sensitive to any kind of impulse that would set it into vibration and Stockhausen was keen to replicate what he could hear close on to the instrument:

> This tam-tam (gong) was hanging in my garden: I couldn't put it in the living room, it was too large. Every once in a while, when I went out for a walk in the garden, I would take a pen or a key, scratch it, or just knock it with my finger, bang it with a pebble, write on it with the pebble, and then often lean my ear very close to the surface of the tam-tam, where I would hear all sorts of strange sound vibrations. At a distance of four or five inches away from the surface, these sounds were no longer audible.[9]

So the composer asked his electronic studio technician to bring over a microphone, band-pass filter and potentiometer. While the technician improvised with the filter and potentiometer, Stockhausen played the tam-tam with a variety of objects from his kitchen and moved the microphone in a range of motions and different directions from the tam-tam. In his inimitable style, Stockhausen's graphic score for *Mikrophonie I* calls for three players: one player 'exciting' the tam-tam with many different objects; a 'microphonist' who makes 'prescribed' movements with a microphone around the surface of the gong; and a live mixer player, using two band-pass filters and potentiometers to shape the overall sound, much like a Jamaican 'dub' mixer would do. Like many of his famous graphic scores, the notation is a vectored tablature, indicating the speed and shape of gong excitations and microphone movements. It also shows the player how to change the potentiometer and filter settings during the performance. The very title of the piece signals the centrality of the microphone as instrument and subject of the composition.

The sound of *Mikrophonie I* is striking in the variety of sound events coaxed from the gong. A polyphony of metallic rustlings and animal-like vocalizations gradually give way to the more resonant pitch sounds, drum hits and singing sounds. When the gong sounds in more traditional ways, it is often modified drastically by the performer with the mixing system.

Stockhausen was absolutely fascinated with the microphone's instrumentality:

> What we are actually doing is listening to a tam-tam . . . like a doctor with a stethoscope listening to the body of a person . . . Someone said, must it be a tam-tam? I said no, I can imagine the score being used to examine an old Volkswagen musically . . . Play anything. Discover the micro-world of the acoustic vibrations, amplify it and transform it electronically.[10]

Whereas Stockhausen used the microphone as a sonic 'stethoscope' in *Mikrophonie I*, other composers began to experiment with the particular acoustic properties of the microphone as it collected and transformed sound in specific acoustical environments.

In 1964 Robert Ashley presented a composition called *The Wolfman* at Charlotte Moorman's Avant Garde Festival of New York. *The Wolfman* came about because Morton Feldman had been asked to compose a solo voice piece, but declined, turning the commission over to Ashley, who used it as an occasion to further his experimentation with the voice:

> I had been thinking about feedback as a sound source for a couple of years, but I had never had the occasion to finish a piece. With Feldman's invitation I jumped into action, knowing full well that the singer would never do the piece I had in mind. Of course, the singer never performed the composition and so I did the first performance.[11]

Ashley's technique was rather low-tech. He simply made close-miked vocal sounds through a sound system simultaneously with a tape composition, and controlled the feedback by putting his mouth up against the microphone. The resulting sound disembodied the performer's voice, lifting it away from its humanness. Although the piece is called *The Wolfman*, the quality of this new voice is mysterious. As Ashley wrote, the result was 'so overpowering to the listener that no one ever understands how the sound is made'.[12]

A few years later, the score was published in *Source* magazine. By this time, the piece had become notorious because of its loud and monolithic sound. Listeners imagined a human performer screaming into the microphone. Ashley was quick and emphatic to argue against the ways his composition was understood in humanistic terms:

Reviewers, listeners and, indeed, some interpreters, I have
been told, have understood *The Wolfman* as a person 'screaming into the microphone'. This couldn't be farther from
the truth. The vocal sounds in the performance have to be
probably the softest vocal sounds ever performed in public ...
The technical idea of the variety of vocal sounds, which doesn't
include any sound above normal speech level, is that the vocal
sounds mix with the feedback (and mix with the sounds of the
tape composition) to create the illusion of spatial movement
to all parts of the hall for the different ingredients of the mix,
depending on frequency and other factors.[13]

In Ashley's musical thinking, the personhood of the voice has
been replaced by the power of the microphone to erase and
dominate vocal production.

Another exploration of the microphone apart from the
human body imagined it moving autonomously in space. With
simplicity and elegance, Steve Reich's *Pendulum Music* uses
gravity and oscillation to make an entire composition from
microphonic feedback. Reich discovered the microphone as a
feedback instrument by accident when working in New Mexico
in 1968:

I had one of these Wollensack tape recorders – they're these
funky 1950s models with a cheap electric microphone. It was
an old machine by then. I had been holding the microphone,
which was plugged into the back of the machine so it could
record. The speaker was turned up. Being out West, I let it
swing back and forth like a lasso. As it passed by the speaker
of the machine, it went 'whoop!' and then it went away.[14]

When it was done as a concert piece at the Whitney
Museum in 1969, during an event of my music, it was 'performed' by Bruce Nauman, Michael Snow, Richard Sierra,

James Tenney and myself. They pulled back their measured microphones and I counted off 4–4 and on the downbeat, they all let it go and sat down, including me. Then the microphones begin to 'whoop!' as they pass in front of the speaker because the microphones had been preset to be loud enough to give feedback when it's in front of the speaker but not when it swings to the left and the right. Over a period of ten minutes, which was a little too long for my taste, and as the pendulums come to rest, you entered a pulsing drone. Once it hit the drone, I would pull the plug on the machine and the whole thing ended.[15]

Composer Alvin Lucier's two most famous compositions, *I Am Sitting in a Room* (1969) and *Music for Solo Performer* (1965) introduced other concepts of feedback, room feedback known as 'standing waves', and brain feedback, the most human feedback imaginable.

In *Music for Solo Performer* (1965), Lucier amplified his own alpha brainwaves (8–12.5 Hz) and played them through loudspeakers connected to a large array of percussion instruments. Lucier had electrodes attached to his forehead, and sat before the audience while controlling his alpha rhythms to create the actual percussion performance.

Composer Richard Teitelbaum, a leading member of the groundbreaking electronic ensemble Musica Elettronica Viva (MEV), incorporated biofeedback and more into his electronic compositions using the Moog synthesizer in the late 1960s.[16] In Teitelbaum's quadraphonic composition *In-tune* (1969), the two performers' EEG electrodes are filtered and then connected to an envelope follower, a device which translates the amplitude changes to a continuous control voltage as well as a gate every time it detects a new amplitude rise. The control voltage drives the frequency of two oscillators of the Moog that are mixed with the performer's voices, while the gates create the actual moment-to-moment sound events of the piece. The singers' breathing and heartbeats are also amplified and are routed to a separate set of speakers. Teitelbaum's piece is best described as a bio-signal composition, since the composer used biofeedback, breath and heartbeats as the primary controlling elements in the music.

Alvin Lucier also realized that acoustical spaces themselves could produce a kind of feedback with the intervention of the microphone, amplifiers and audio recording devices. In *I Am Sitting in a Room*, Lucier reads and records a short text that will be used to cause a room to feed back. Standing waves cause certain frequencies in a room to remain fixed while others resonate and are thus louder. The dimensions and physical shape of a space will determine these frequencies, and they are calculable. However, one can easily find them unscientifically simply by singing at different frequencies – room resonances are quite easy to hear. In Lucier's piece, the text is both the sonic material for the piece and the score:

> I am sitting in a room different from the one you are in now. I am recording the sound of my speaking voice and I am going to play it back into the room again and again until the resonant frequencies of the room reinforce themselves so that any semblance of my speech, with perhaps the exception of rhythm, is destroyed. What you will hear, then, are the natural resonant frequencies of the room articulated by speech. I regard this activity not so much as a demonstration of a physical fact, but more as a way to smooth out any irregularities my speech might have.[17]

By first recording the text, and then playing it back in a room and re-recording it each time, Lucier created a process where the resonant frequencies of the room (nodal frequencies created by standing waves that are determined by the room's dimensions) will gradually become louder and louder in relation to the loudness of the composer's voice on the original recording. The room thus begins to 'ring' at the resonant frequencies while the voice becomes more and more submerged in the texture. It is his stuttering speech rhythms (impulses) that cause the room to resonate, while the multiple re-recordings cause feedback. As each re-recording is played back, what initially sounds like a person speaking gradually fades down to nothing. The composer's speech is gradually replaced by a floating, chordal, flute-like sound space.

Lucier describes another feedback composition, this one using a feedback system made up of small, individual resonant spaces to create feedback events:

> for several years I had a specific idea about exploring the acoustic properties of certain gamelan instruments . . . I thought of the bonangs, bronze bowl-like gongs of various sizes, as small environments, the resonant frequencies of which could be revealed. By inserting microphones into the cavities of these instruments and bringing the amplifier gain up to the level of feedback the resonant frequencies would sound.[18]

A late 1980s 'home studio' tour posted on YouTube shows Laurie Anderson in her preferred working environment. The composer and multimedia artist demonstrates her brilliant use of the microphone coupled to various signal-processed personas, such as the gender-changing downward pitch-shifted voice of 'authority', her harmonized 'back-up singers from boxes', as she refers to them, and long echoed versions of herself. She is remarkable for incorporating the Roland VP-330 vocoder and looped voice on her electro-minimalist 1981 hit single 'O Superman'. Recorded in a hallway in her apartment building, it was originally released on a small label, but then found its way to John Peel's radio show in England. After re-release on the Warner Brothers label, it reached No. 2 on the UK singles chart. 'The song is based around a looped "ha ha ha ha" done on a harmoniser, but I wanted it to be like a Greek chorus – not just one voice – so I used a vocoder,' explained Anderson in an interview.[19] Her incorporation of harmonizers, pitch-shifters and vocoders became the underpinning of her vocal work in the 1980s. For her, these devices, but especially the vocoder, allowed her to leave her body: 'I want to feel empathy and be able to go into another person's position . . . With vocoders I like being able to be a little bit removed . . . I don't always have to be myself, which can be pretty tiring.'[20]

It is, perhaps, counter-intuitive to imagine the sound environment as itself a musical instrument, but that was in effect the case in these compositions. We tend to think of the sound environment as a kind of neutral context, unless we stop to re-conceptualize it in a way that credits its ability to shape, colour and design our ways of hearing. Although this pivot towards the environment has been understood in terms of aesthetics or taste, I prefer to understand the trajectory of electronic music as continuing along more pragmatic and materialist lines.

R. Murray Schafer's important book *The Tuning of the World* (1977), introduced new notions of archival and ecological practice to what he termed 'the soundscape' – the acoustic environment of particular places and geographies. His work began to give theoretical and conceptual weight to the idea of the soundscape as an ongoing musical composition.

As Schafer became more and more interested in environment and sound, he began to develop a basic, useful lexicon. Schafer's theories of keynote sounds, signals and soundmarks are fundamental examples of his tools for the study of soundscapes.[21] A keynote sound, in its most general sense, is the sound of a particular place, a kind of background or ambient tonality. Signal sounds to him were basically foreground sounds, like alarms, whistles, sirens and so on, that demanded attention. The 'soundmark' is the most interesting term in his lexicon. Derived from the concept of the landmark, the soundmark is a regular sonic occurrence that uniquely defines a particular geography. For instance, imagine someone's daily life in a place like Niagara Falls, New York, where the water's thunderous sound envelops the inhabitants for miles around. Schafer himself, who lives in Vancouver, may have had in mind its constant harbour activity as an example of a soundmark. Although Schafer's descriptive terms may seem rather simple, in retrospect their compositional inspiration was conceptually advanced.

Like so many musical thinkers, Schafer owed much to John Cage, whose 4'33" was the crucial influence in developing the notion of the soundscape. Each performance of Cage's famous 'silent composition' frames the instantaneous ambient sound field in such a way as to invite/force the listener to hear sounds – any sounds – as music. The listener is invited/forced to hear the instantaneous ambient sound field in a fluid state, a state of constant 'becoming'.[22] Cage's piece is critical in the way it liberated the ear of the listener, and by extension the microphone, to hear the world musically.

Luc Ferrari's *Presque rien*, discussed earlier, represented the first field recording with a musical aesthetic. Ferrari made only minimal interventions as far as tape techniques were concerned. His editing really amounted to a simple compression of time – he recorded every day at the same time, then seamlessly edited the recurring mundane activities from three hours to just under twenty minutes.

In an entirely different mode than that of the highly conceptual Cage, Ferrari proceeded empirically. Instead of self-consciously abstracting the source material of *Presque rien*, this recorded 'reality' becomes a prompt for the listener to make sonic connections to their own conscious and unconscious processes. Ferrari's idea of the 'anecdote' and its concomitant 'ambiguities' might well be defined as a real-time flow of analogies, or a constellation of sound analogies. Constellations of sound analogies allow relationships – both similarities and differences – to emerge with the listener, rather than being directed by the composer. Ferrari's composition remains an unexpected turn towards likeness and realism during a time of highly complex and abstract musical thinking. The present-day practices of sound art and field recording owe a great deal to Ferrari's realist aesthetic.

These new sound practices present a range of listening challenges. The microphone and recording/amplification process decouples the sound-object from its source, removes it from time and space, changes its dynamic profile and thus begs for new ways of listening.

Ultimately, Pierre Schaeffer's acousmatic listening project seemed too dogmatic in its prohibition of subjective reference to sounds. In contrast, Ola Stockfelt's theory of adequate modes of listening brings the listener a more generous range of competencies, suggesting that genres develop over time with listening groups.

In 1998 the biologist and sound artist Francisco López released a composition entitled *La Selva: Sound Environments from a Neotropical Rain Forest*. In the accompanying CD booklet, López included an essay in which he promotes a 'profound listening' practice:

> I believe in the possibility of a profound, pure, 'blind' listening
> of sounds, freed (as much as possible) of procedural, context-
> ual or intentional levels of reference. What is more important,
> I conceive this as an ideal form of transcendental listening that
> doesn't deny at all what is outside the sounds but explores and
> affirms all what is inside them. This purist, absolute concep-
> tion is an attempt at fighting against the dissipation of this
> inner world.[23]

López notes that while bioacoustics generally attempts to
capture the various animal species by acoustically fore-
grounding them, his method of recording *La Selva* did not
attempt to distinguish foreground and background, but simply
whatever was happening at the time of the recording. He points
out that there is always an unavoidable privileging of sound
events due to the microphone placement, but still wishes the
listening to focus on the 'sound environment as a whole'.[24]

López also raises an objection to the general sense of
hearing a natural space as a classification based on its animal-
generated sound. Instead, he groups the non-biotic sounds such
as wind, rain and water along with animal and insect sounds
with a category that is not often really heard in field recordings
– plants and trees:

> If our perspective of nature sounds were more focused on the
> environment as a whole, instead of on behavioral manifest-
> ations of the organisms we foresee as most similar to us, we
> could also deal with plant bioacoustics. Furthermore, a sound
> environment is not only the consequence of all its sound-
> producing components, but also of all its sound-transmitting
> and sound-modifying elements. The birdsong we hear in the
> forest is as much a consequence of the bird as of the trees or
> the forest floor. If we are really listening, the topography, the

degree of humidity of the air or the type of materials in the topsoil are as essential and definitory as the sound-producing animals that inhabit a certain space.[25]

Although López reveals much about the capacity of the microphone to gather sound, his most radical claim is the assignment of meaning and appreciation to the listener:

I believe in an expansion and transformation of our concept of music through nature (as through 'non-nature' in the sense expressed above). This doesn't mean an absolute assignment of sounds to music . . . Instead, it refers to my belief that music is an aesthetic (in its widest sense) perception/understanding/conception of sound. It's our decision – subjective, intentional, non-universal, not necessarily permanent what converts nature sounds into music.[26]

The new sonic surfaces of the world that the microphone has revealed have given it a new status as a multivalent, layered, complex ear on the world. The microphone has made us privy to a whole range of sound events that – more and more – we are able to hear with a fullness of meaning.

Western music philosophy has long entertained the idea of the natural world producing its own music. The music of the spheres is, perhaps, the most familiar formulation of a musical cosmology. The notion of celestial harmony as the ideal of music influenced many famous musical treatises. Electronic music has, on the other hand, not worked from musical universals or ideals, developing instead from more pragmatic and experimental premises. As such, electronic music composers have necessarily approached the natural world as a series of partial and changing soundscapes that are discovered and/or generated by the microphone.

Holly Herndon performs at 40 Watt Club on 27 March 2015 in Athens, Georgia.

5
COMPUTERS

Music, both in theory and in practice, has long been associated with mathematics. With this in mind, let us begin with the modest proposition that music and computers are analogous. Given the systematic elements of music theory and music's numeric representation from the time of the Greeks to the present day, it was only a question of time before someone seized upon their manifest affinities.

In the mid-1950s a chemist turned composer, Lejaren Hiller, began to see the logic and decision-making abilities of the computer as a tool for composing music. Computers at this time, even though blazingly fast compared to human calculations, were still far too slow to generate sound itself. However, Hiller realized that the computer could be programmed to write notes and rhythms that later could be translated into traditional music notation.

Hiller's premise, based on common-practice harmony and counterpoint, was that since music is 'governed by laws of organization which permit fairly exact codification, the computer might be used to "create a random universe" and to select ordered set of information in accordance with imposed rules'. He further surmised that since the composer's task could be 'similarly viewed as an imposition of order upon an infinite variety of possibilities', there was 'an analogy between the two processes'.[1]

Hiller tested his hypotheses with his own compositional practice. His work on the *Illiac Suite* for string quartet focused on working with an a priori set of compositional rules. It is useful to think of these as similar to syntactic rules in linguistics. Working from Fux's *Gradus ad Parnassum*, a practical course in sixteenth-century counterpoint, he programmed a computer to generate *cantus firmi* – diatonic melodies. His aim was to subsequently program the computer to write new melodies against each *cantus firmus*, creating combinations of simultaneous melodies that would produce acceptable consonances and dissonances according to the rules of counterpoint.[2]

In programming terms, he employed what was known as the 'Monte Carlo Method'. This method relied on the computer to randomly generate millions of integers, representing diatonic pitches, and then apply laws of probability theory to narrow down the possibilities that tested 'true' according to traditional counterpoint rules. As Hiller explains:

> In the first operation, the computer was instructed to generate random sequences of integers which were equated to the notes of the musical scale ... These random integers ... were then processed in the second, more complex operation in which each random integer was screened through a series of arithmetic tests expressing various rules of composition and either used or rejected depending on which rules were in effect. If accepted, the random integer was used to build up a 'composition' and stored in the computer until the completed 'composition' was ready to be printed out. On the other hand, if it was rejected, a new random integer was generated and examined. This process was repeated until a satisfactory note

was found or until it became evident that no such note existed, in which case part of the 'composition' thus far composed was automatically erased to allow a fresh start.[3]

The *Illiac Suite* for string quartet comprised four movements, which Hiller called 'Experiments'. 'Experiment One' used a limited selection of species counterpoint rules to create monody, two-part and four-part textures using *cantus firmi* from three to twelve notes in length. 'Experiment Two' began with four-part random diatonic music that was gradually sculpted with the application of first species counterpoint rules. 'Experiment Three' used randomly generated chromatic pitches with correlated control of rhythm, dynamics and articulations. The movement closed with the use of tone-rows and transpositions. 'Experiment Four' was an exploration of 'Markoff chain' music. Based on the laws of probability, a Markoff chain is a series of interlocked computer 'decisions', in which 'the choice of each new event can be made dependent on previous events.' Thus the progression from one pitch to the next is 'weighted', with one note more likely than another according to preset odds.

Whereas Hiller's work influenced musicological work in computer 'style analysis', the Greek composer and architect Iannis Xenakis profoundly influenced what we now generally refer to as 'algorithmic composition'. Xenakis's work represents a highly developed line of thinking. Xenakis was more concerned with using computations to create large-scale sound structures, with possibilities of different smaller-scale outcomes. Xenakis used various computational techniques to compose both music for acoustic instruments – transcribed to musical notation as Hiller did – and computer-generated sound, as the technology became available.

In the preface to his book *Formalized Music*, Xenakis describes his musical thinking as analogous to scientific thought, calling it 'the effort to make "art" while "geo-metrizing," that is, by giving it reasoned support less perishable than the impulse of the moment'.[4] Taste was no longer relevant:

> For this purpose the qualification 'beautiful' or 'ugly' makes no sense for sound, nor for the music that derives from it; the quantity of intelligence carried by the sounds must be the true criterion of the validity of a particular music.[5]

This aesthetic position runs counter to every commonly held notion about 'beauty' in music. Still, there are precedents.

Milton Babbitt, for instance, had suggested something very similar in an article originally published in *High Fidelity* magazine in 1958 with the provocative title (added by the editor) 'Who Cares if You Listen?':

> The time has passed when the normally well-educated man without special preparation could understand the most advanced work in, for example, mathematics, philosophy, and physics. Advanced music, to the extent that it reflects the knowledge and originality of the informed composer, scarcely can be expected to appear more intelligible than these arts and sciences . . .[6]

These striking claims are, in turn, akin to Cage's plea to 'let sounds be themselves'.[7] This famous quotation is, quite rightly, often associated with Cage's ideas of subverting the compositional will of the composer, but could it also suggest that he believed that sounds carried with them an inherent 'intelligence'? Edgard Varèse, speaking about the electronic music medium in 1962, touched a similar nerve: 'I should like you to consider what I believe is the best definition of music, because it is all-inclusive: "the corporealization of the intelligence that is in sound," as proposed by Hoene Wronsky.'[8]

Xenakis's stochastic music used 'probabilistic logic' as a way of vastly expanding something like a serial composition's 'deterministic causality' in such a way that serialism would be only one of many possibilities of generating music.[9] Xenakis also describes his desire to model nature:

> natural events such as the collision of hail or rain with hard surfaces, or the song of cicadas in a summer field. These sonic events are made out of thousands of isolated sounds; this multitude of sounds, seen as a totality is a new sonic event . . . which itself follows aleatory and stochastic laws.[10]

Thus Xenakis's idea is of a musical structure where 'note' or 'not-note' are equally valid, ontologically speaking. Despite coming from an entirely different aesthetic reasoning, this Zen notion is distinctly Cageian.

By 1978 Xenakis was developing his UPIC computer system, which could translate graphical images into sound. The composer, who had initially practised architecture, began to experiment with his hand-made drawings as the actual scores for sound synthesis. The drawing is scaled into time and pitch events. Rather than following the idea of the performer-interpretable intent of many of the graphic scores of the 1960s avant-garde composers, the UPIC system was much more literal – up was higher-pitched, down was lower-pitched, time flowed fron left to right and so on.

Mycenae Alpha was the first of these pieces he created using UPIC. It is clustered and noisy, rather crude compared to a composition written about ten years later using the UPIC system, *Voyage absolu des Unari vers Andromède* (1989). The dense thicket of tones and noise is counterpointed with various sharper events. The piece has a definite programmatic element, suggesting a sense of deep space flight. This futuristic piece was produced using the most ancient representational gesture – the human hand with a plain tool.

Neither *Voyage absolu des Unari vers Andromède*, with its forward-looking, graphic interface, nor any other single compositional advancement constituted a momentous or definitive split from earlier technology. Histories of technology often tend to exaggerate these breaks. In electronic music, there have never been clear boundaries between analogue and digital practices. For example, the RCA Mark II synthesizer was controlled digitally by what amounted to player piano rolls. Player piano rolls were mass-produced mechanical tablatures that simply marked the places of notes, more storage units than anything else. What is interesting here is that the player piano was also a hybrid, digital/analogue instrument.

Milton Babbitt saw in this interface a deeper complexity and usefulness:

> The Mark II provides for the production of and the measurable and regulable control of these components of the musical event: frequency, envelope, spectrum, intensity, duration, and of the mode of progression from such an event to the following event. This control resides in the programming input of the Synthesizer, where the properties of these components are specified in the form of binary code instructions, holes punched in a fifteen-inch wide paper roll by keys, mounted on a keyboard and arranged in ten vertical columns of four keys each.[11]

One encounters many of these kinds of analogue-digital hybridizations throughout the history of electronic music.

Main Frames and Corporations

After these exploratory beginnings, it was clear that computer sound generation required more than individual initiative. Because of the number of calculations per second needed to generate sound, it was not until the era of the mainframe computer that substantial progress could be made. This required a large influx of capital but also, just as importantly, the continued participation of very talented musicians and engineers.

The representation of sound by a computer is accomplished by sampling. Sound waves are continuous by nature, but a computer must store them as a series of discrete numbers (samples) that only approximate the original sound wave. The concept is quite similar in film, where a series of still images moves fast enough to 'trick' the eye and the brain into the perception of continuous motion. It takes approximately 25 frames per second to produce this effect in film or video. The ear is much more discriminating, requiring approximately 45,000 samples per second to reproduce a continuous sound wave clearly. So, the representation of sound requires both fast computation times and a large amount of computer memory.

Max Mathews was an electrical engineer working at Bell Laboratories in Murray Hill, New Jersey in the mid-1950s. Though the Australian CSIRAC computer system was able to play rudimentary melodies in the early 1950s, Mathews is responsible for the first concentrated work in computer sound synthesis. It was an arduous process. Early on, Mathews had to generate a computer tape at IBM Headquarters in New York City, then travel the 30 miles (48 km) back to Bell Labs to convert the computer sound samples back to analogue sound. By 1957 his program Music I could generate monophonic melodies with triangle wave and, by the next year, Music II featured four channels of sound and sixteen different waveforms.

The various iterations and offshoots over the next 25 years had a similar modular synthesis architecture. These programs are actually collections of sub-programs that model oscillators, filters, envelope functions and waveforms. The user builds an 'instrument' connected with virtual patch cords. The next stage is to write a 'score', which calls particular instruments to play specific sound events described by notes, durations, amplitudes and other parameters specified in the instrument design (for example, frequency modulation). In the early years, composers used punch cards, and then moved to computer terminals.

In addition to allowing composers to do additive synthesis and subtractive synthesis much more easily, the mainframe computer programs allowed the development of new types of synthesis. This was costly. Mainframe computer time was charged by the hour, and composers using the new software were often only allowed to run jobs in the middle of the night. So an initial challenge of mainframe synthesis was to find efficient algorithms, which don't take a lot of computation to generate rich sound palettes.

Bell Labs, the primary corporate entity in the development of sound synthesis, recognized the importance of having creative thinkers and composers in residence. In 1961 the multi-talented young composer James Tenney came to Bell Labs to work for three years in psychoacoustics and computer music. His influence was inestimable. Tenney's *Analog No. 1: Noise Study*, composed using Music III the same year he came to Bell Labs, is credited as being the first piece of computer music composed by a trained composer. Inspired by the sounds of traffic as he commuted from New York City to Bell Labs, Tenney began to imagine how he might generate those ambient sounds with a computer. He experimented with a noise unit-generator and the ways in which it 'could start narrow-band and go to wide-band or start soft and go loud or low and go high. *Noise Study* was dependent on that possibility.'[12] Relying on noise unit-generators that are shaped by filters and amplitude modulation, Tenney's piece features a striking use of continuously changing, organic bands of noise. This stunning piece remains as one of the best, early examples of computer music. As a brilliant musical thinker, Tenney also contributed important theoretical work in the study of musical timbre while at Bell Labs. Tenney was very interested in musical timbre and published a model that was based on three large areas – the steady-state spectrum, the quasi-steady-state modulation processes, and the non-steady-state, transient phenomena.

A series of other talented musicians were recruited by Bell. The French composer Jean-Claude Risset came to work at Bell Labs in 1964. His work also focused on the study of musical timbre, particularly brass instruments. Risset is known for his important computer music compositions like 'Mutations', which uses frequency modulation synthesis, and his intricate 'Sheppard-Risset tones' – a barber's pole effect where a tone of rising or falling frequency never seems to reach its destination.

Composer Laurie Spiegel is credited with creating a large number of important and well-known compositions during her years at Bell Labs. Her work is minimalist in one sense, but eclectic and rich in its timbral constructions. She cites both John Fahey and J. S. Bach as major influences on her work. She composed a number of important pieces between 1974 and 1977 using the GROOVE system developed by Max Mathews and F. R. Moore at Bell Labs, including 'Patchwork', the 'Appalachian Grove' series and 'Kepler's Harmony of the Worlds', chosen for inclusion on the golden record in the payload of the Voyager space probe. The GROOVE program provided Spiegel with unprecedented real-time interaction in her compositions.

Computer Music and the University

Princeton University, located in close proximity to Bell Labs, established an important working relationship with the lab that continued throughout the 1960s and '70s. Mathews shared the program with the Princeton Music Department and with other institutions that were interested in exploring it. Mathews had developed Music IV for the IBM 7094 computer and it happened that Princeton also had a 7094. The resulting creative synergy between Bell Labs and Princeton was explosive. Princeton composers Godfrey Winham and Hubert Howe began working with the program while making some changes to it. They called their version Music IVB. Howe notes appreciatively that

> Music 4B was an elegantly written program. I learned a lot by studying the code written by Joan Miller, the person who wrote most of it. In those days, program efficiency was paramount, and we learned how to write very tight programs. We liked what Music 4 did, but the program was awkward to use and required lots of unnecessary typing . . . [W]e immediately began to revise aspects of Music 4 and ultimately created what we called Music 4B. One of the first things we did was to revise the score, introducing the carry feature and the octave point pitch class notation. We also developed many new unit generators, including SLOPE and EXPON, Godfrey's FORMNT, digital filtering, and artificial reverberation, which came later, after Godfrey learned about John Chowning's work.[13]

In the interest of making this software more than a technical contrivance, the Princeton composer J. K. Randall raised key musical questions for the next stages of Music IV. In this generous collaborative context, he composed his most important works, *Mudgett* and *Lyric Variations for Violin and*

Computer. Howe recalls that he, Winham and Randall discussed 'very practical issues', such as how accelerandi and ritardandi could be programmed, computer-friendly concepts of pitch notation, and smoother programming of glissandi.[14]

Music IV was written in Fortran, and since this language was so accessible, the program began to find its way into universities and other laboratories. Hubert Howe rewrote Music IVB by himself in 1966–7 in Fortran as Music 4BF. He and Winham expanded the program further, with the intent to make it 'more intelligible and intuitive for musicians'.[15]

One interesting musical development from Princeton in the area of timbre was Winham's FORMNT unit generator that could generate both harmonic and inharmonic partials. We often associate inharmonic spectra with classes of sounds such as drums, gongs and other random metallic sounds. Harmonic spectra comprise most acoustic instrumental sounds, such as those of winds, strings and brass. Another timbral development was J. K. Randall's subprogram that would, among other things, map 'basic sets of [harmonic] partials onto enlarged and compressed spaces'.[16] This musical idea was exciting because it suggested a new way to link instrumental timbre with computer-generated sound spectra.

In 1965 the violinist Paul Zukofsky commissioned J. K. Randall's *Lyric Variations for Violin and Computer*. Designed as a conventional tape composition with Zukofsky's parts recorded in a studio, it is one of the early masterpieces of the new genre. The twenty variations are highly structured interactions between the violin and computer. Randall states:

> Throughout the computer part, I have tried to impose upon conventionally peripheral aspects of sound (vibrato, tremolo, reverberation, waveform transformation, etc.) the same degree of elaborate structuring that I impose (and

that any composer imposes) upon pitch, attack-rhythm, and duration.[17]

Randall's remarkable piece is characterized by a seamless integration of timbres that are convincing examples of how suited mainframe computer synthesis was to the aesthetics of serialism applied to timbre construction. Randall almost militantly describes this structuring, saying that

the listener ought provisionally to lay aside the obsolete and vague notion of 'timbre' – a bushel basket for whatever aspects of sound we may in the past have relegated (however mistakenly) to the role of subliminally 'lushing-up' pitch-production – and ought instead to follow the individual participation of such aspects in the unfolding of the piece.[18]

By the 1970s Princeton had established itself as one of the most renowned music departments in the world, producing a new generation of students and teachers committed to computer music. The departmental faculty recruited their postgraduate students from the most prestigious traditional music conservatories and university music departments and established a rigorous and experimental programme that set the standard for computer music education.

As part of a new generation of postgraduate students and teachers, Princeton composer Paul Lansky began working in computer music in the early 1970s. His 1973 computer piece *Mild und Leise* (Mildly and Gently) is lush and romantic while at the same time it uses a structured approach to the correlation of pitch and musical timbre, much in the spirit of Milton Babbitt's compositions done on the RCA Synthesizer and Randall's work with Music IV. The title was drawn from the opening lines of the *Liebestod* (love-death), in the final act of Wagner's *Tristan und Isolde*. The composer described the working process:

> I used the Music360 computer language written by Barry Vercoe. This IBM mainframe was, as far as I know, the only computer on the Princeton University campus at the time. It had about one megabyte of memory, and cost hundreds of thousands of dollars (in addition to requiring a staff to run it around the clock). At that point we were actually using punch cards to communicate with the machine, and writing the output to a 1600 BPI digital tape which we then had to carry over to a lab in the basement of the engineering quadrangle in order to listen to it.[19]

As for the music, Lansky explains: 'The pitch and timbre arrays would work in parallel. At the source, which was the "Tristan chord" and its inversion, I would have a very simple timbre. As the cycles folded outward, the timbres would become more and more complex.'[20]

Lansky became interested in speech synthesis partly as a refusal of the traditional text-setting process of composers:

> I had tried writing songs and I felt that, for me, setting a text was a sort of arbitrary and pointless act . . . So I decided I would use the machine to deal with this issue. If I had just written a piece for soprano and piano, I had the feeling I would reinvent someone else's wheel. To deal with this I decided to write a piece in which the sound of speech was to become a musical object. This was the *Six Fantasies on a Poem by Thomas Campion* [1979].[21]

Lansky's interest was a result of having new digital control over recorded sound. He has said that he was always put off by the traditional tape techniques of *musique concrète*:

> I found early on that the spirit and sense of musique concrète
> was fascinating, challenging, and provocative. I thought it was
> very much worth investigating, however, I really didn't like
> analog tape technology . . . I'm strictly a second-generation
> electronic musician.[22]

It may be hard for some contemporary electronic musicians
to imagine the sheer number of hours of labour involved in
producing both early tape compositions and computer sound
synthesis; for the next wave of computer music composers
like Lansky, the speed and ease of digital editing and sound
processing was liberating, and in Lansky's case drew him to
reconsider what was at the time an antiquated *musique concrète*
compositional aesthetic.[23]

Commerce and the Computer

It was inevitable that mainframe computer music composition
would soon become obsolete. By the 1980s, developments in
computer speed, memory and miniaturization pointed towards
smaller and more personally friendly devices. The story of
the DX7 is a remarkable example of this changeover from
large hardware to a portable and powerful digital synthesizer.
Running MUSIC V at Stanford University in 1967, composer John
Chowning's experiments with digital frequency modulation led
to a discovery of a powerful synthesis technique now known as
linear FM. Chowning explains:

> I was experimenting with very rapid and deep vibrato [a music
> effect characterized by a rapid, pulsating change in pitch]. As
> I increased the vibrato in speed and depth, I realized I was no
> longer hearing instant pitch and time.

So, at slower rates, frequency modulation approximates what we call vibrato in an acoustic instrument or voice, the slight rhythmic changing of pitch slightly above and below a note in question. Using electronic or computer means, speeding up the 'modulation rate' into the audio range produces 'sidebands', new frequencies that can be harmonically or non-harmonically related depending on the frequency ratios of the carrier and modulator. If the two frequencies are set at integral multiples of each other, the resulting spectrum is harmonic; otherwise a wide variety of inharmonic spectra are possible.

Chowning's 1977 crystalline composition *Stria* is a working through of his interest in FM synthesis, particularly the use of inharmonically generated sound spectra. According to the composer 'several levels of the piece are governed by the ratio of the Golden Mean', such as its timbral construction.[24]

Chowning's FM techniques were used by other classical composers with access to mainframe synthesis studios, but his desire to make the technology portable and relatively affordable was slow going. Hammond, Wurlitzer and Lowry, the three main U.S. organ companies, all turned down the idea. However, a young engineer from the Yamaha Corporation saw the commercial possibilities, since the company was already exploring digital applications in music.

After several years of experimentation and prototypes, Yamaha engineers finally succeeded in implementing FM synthesis on an Intel 3000 chip. The instrument, called the DX7, was released in 1983 and was an instant success. The $2,000 instrument was portable, though a bit heavy, had sixteen-note polyphony, stored 32 user patches (sounds) in addition to the internal presets, and was quite revolutionary in terms of the range of musicians who used it: Beastie Boys, Phil Collins, Chick Corea, The Cure, Depeche Mode, Brian Eno, Enya, Herbie Hancock, Elton John, Kraftwerk, Lynyrd Skynyrd, Robert Palmer,

Queen, Supertramp, Talking Heads, Toto, U2, Steve Winwood, Stevie Wonder and Yes.

Canned sounds in digital synthesizers have always been musically problematic. The DX7 was no different in this regard, as its sonic possibilities were vastly underutilized. The 'factory' patches ended up defining the main musical character of the instrument that was capable of much more.

Other Synthesis Techniques

Following some of the initial implications of Xenakis's stochastic compositions, Curtis Roads's work on granular synthesis has provided a deep, enduring reservoir of sonic possibility in computer music composition. Roads cites Xenakis's statement that 'all sound is an integration of grains, of elementary sonic particles, of sonic quanta'[25] as a beginning point for his work to implement granular synthesis using Music V. As he points out, the 'instrument used to produce an individual grain may be quite simple', with each grain having controllable waveform, frequency and amplitude.[26] The synthesized sound is composed by adding these elementary units to form 'clouds', where start time, duration, density, bandwidth and amplitude shape can be specified. Roads's work with this atomization of sound has spread, with granular synthesis now used to both create and manipulate sound, but also to digitally process it for purposes of time stretching and compression, pitch-shifting, delay and reverberation.

Waveshaping is another technique made available by mainframe computer sound synthesis that found its way to portable digital synthesizers. This technique is basically sound synthesis by distortion, not unlike what a fuzz pedal does to a guitar signal. A sine wave is processed by a non-linear function by means of a technique called 'table-lookup'. It is a process of

simply substituting the instantaneous value of the input signal
with a value from the lookup table for that same time instant.
The loudness of the input signal determines how much of the
lookup table is used and as the amplitude increases, more and
more sidebands are generated, thus changing the timbre, as
happens in frequency modulation.

Composer Daniel Arfib's *Le Souffle du doux* (The Whistle of
the Gentle) was composed in 1979. Using the Music V program,
he created extremely slow-changing non-tempered harmonic
landscapes interspersed with bands of pitched noise. The
meditative, evolving harmonics are the result of using the
Chebyshev polynomials as the shaping functions.

Microchip Technology

The last of these foundational 'Music N' mainframe computer
synthesis programs were Music V and Cmusic, with much
creative work done at Pierre Boulez's IRCAM facility in Paris and
at the University of California San Diego.

One of most interesting pieces from IRCAM during this
time is the English composer Jonathan Harvey's *Mortuos
Plango, Vivos Voco* (1980). The sound sources for the
composition were the tenor bell from Winchester Cathedral
and the voice of Harvey's son, then a chorister at the Cathedral.
Harvey used the Music V program to first analyse the bell's
harmonic spectrum, and then to construct new sounds based
on that timbral information. It is an eight-channel piece that
simulates the effect of the listener being inside the bell while
sitting in the concert hall. Each of the eight sections of the
work are based, in turn, on the pitch of the first eight partials
of the bell. Harvey used the frequencies of the higher partials
to generate chordal material for the piece. The composition
is a tour de force of mainframe computer music, combining

traditional bell and vocal sounds, ghostly chords and highly synthetic glissandi.

With the advent of microchip technology and personal computers in the 1980s, things changed drastically. There are now direct descendants of the Music N programs such as MAX/MSP, Pure Data, SuperCollider and Reaktor that offer all of this technology to the laptop user.

Two transitional portable digital synthesizers are notable for their application of mainframe synthesis techniques. Wolfgang Palm's Wavecomputer 360 used waveshaping, along with filters and envelope generators for its sound generation. This was followed in 1981 by the PPG WAVE, and finally the Waldorf Microwave in 1989. These wavetable synthesizers are really unique in terms of sonic possibility and their technology remained underexplored.

The Fairlight CMI became commercially available in 1979, but its huge cost – about $90,000 in today's dollars – meant that most could only imagine its possibilities. Its Australian inventors, Peter Vogel and Kim Ryrie, created the first digital sampling instrument played by a keyboard. It could record sounds directly and map them onto a keyboard. It also had a touch screen controlled by a light pen.

Peter Gabriel is said to have bought the first Fairlight CMI, and the progressive-rock group Yes had one. The group Art of Noise was actually created because of a short drum beat fragment that Gary Langan, J. J. Jeczalik and Anne Dudley re-recorded onto producer Trevor Horn's CMI. The three were working on an album with Yes's album 90125. Langan recalls:

> Because I was the engineer, I was the curator of a tape . . . that YES had scrapped but the drum sound was just absolutely incredible . . . I asked him [J. J. Jeczalik] to sample me a bar because we only had one and a half seconds of sample at the

time, so I reckoned we could just about get a bar in. And J. J.,
bless him, not being very musical made a happy accident of
hitting the 'go' button on beat 3 and not beat 1 of the bar! So
when he played it back to me, I now had this drum groove
that was effectively backwards, it was going '3-4-1-2-3-4-1-2'
and I said 'you're a genius!' And I said 'OK, now let's put some
of those wacky things that we've sampled from when the
Fairlight was living round at my house' because J. J. used to rent
a room from me. The sounds happened to be a guy trying to
start his VW Golf and other bits that we'd had a go at sampling.
So we stuck around that night and did the demo that became
[the single] 'Beat Box'.[27]

These PPG and Fairlight synthesizers were wildly expensive and
were not really viable in the mass market.

The Yamaha DX7 marked the crossover from mainframe,
classical music computer synthesis to the pop, rock and jazz
worlds. A veritable explosion of digital synthesizers followed the
DX7. Interestingly, these digital synthesizers made their way into
popular music because the lower cost of digital technology made
them much more affordable. For the most part, they represent
little, musically speaking. Instead, they are technologies of
musical convenience, featuring things like preset memory, many
factory sounds and, most importantly, polyphonic keyboards.
It was the development of the drum machine and then the
affordable sampler that generated the next wave of new musical
thinking. However, there is one outlier here, one that single-
handedly created a whole new genre of music.

The Roland TB-303

The Roland TB-303 was originally marketed as an 'automatic
bass machine'. It was conceived as an accompaniment tool for

musicians, much in the same way that the original 'rhythm machines' were accompanists for organists. Designed by Roland's Tadao Kikumoto, the TB part of its name stood for 'transistor bass' and it featured analogue sound circuitry and a digital memory. It could store bass lines by specifying pitch, note attack and duration, accent and slide (portamento). It was hard to program and did not sound at all like a bass. Roland ceased production of the unit after a year and a half, with some ten thousand TB-303s made. After that, the TB-303 sank into oblivion.

The TB-303 had a single audio oscillator that could play either a sawtooth or square wave. There was an envelope generator with a decay control, and a Moog-inspired lowpass filter with a 'resonance' control. It was this knob that would give the TB-303 its characteristic sound that would spawn a whole new musical genre in Chicago. DJ (Nathan) Pierre recounts its entry into the Chicago house scene with the song 'Acid Tracks':

> We were trying to find a sound, and we bought keyboards and everything, and nothing kind of clicked with us ... This guy named Jasper G, who was just a friend of ours, made a track, and when I heard his track, I was like 'Yo, what did you use for the bassline?' And he said, 'A Roland TB-303.' We didn't know what that was. I went by his house and I saw it ... but it was just being used for what it was meant to be used for: as a bassline machine.[28]

One of the other members of DJ Pierre's band Phuture found a TB-303 in a second-hand shop for $40. DJ Pierre continues:

> I came over to his house, and he already had a beat plan, but we didn't know how to program it. We had it synched up, and it was playing some stuff, and I started just tweaking knobs and turning stuff, and Spanky was like, 'Woah, woah, woah. Keep

doing that, keep doing that.' So, I kept twisting knobs, and the next thing you know, we were there for like an hour or two, just twisting knobs and programming things. The funny thing is, that first day, we made 'Acid Tracks'. It was quite spiritual, to be honest. It was like, that 303 and I connected, in a way that I had never connected to a piece of equipment before.[29]

DJ Pierre played the raw track for Chicago House master musician Marshall Jefferson. Jefferson suggested they lower the tempo from 128 bpm to 120, and helped do the basic mix for the piece. Released in 1987, the record was a huge success in Chicago and the UK, and its futuristic sound began to be called 'acid house'.

'Give the Drummer (Machine) Some'

The drum machine had a singular importance because it created a whole set of genres of beat-oriented music that continues to the present day, including hip-hop, house, techno, electronica and virtually all of pop music. The technique of laying down a drum machine track and then composing a song to it is nothing new in musical history. The technique of successive counterpoint is found in sixteenth-century polyphony, for example Morales's *Missa de Beata Virgine*. Many composers, including Haydn and Beethoven, trained as composers by using J. J. Fux's *Gradus as Parnassum*, a species counterpoint book based on the practice of writing successive counterpoint against a given melodic line, the *cantus firmus*. In this case of the drum machine, the *cantus firmus* is not a chant melody, but a rhythmic pattern. Amazingly enough, the person we have to thank for this groundbreaking development began by trying to make an instrument that would be an 'accompanist' to the amateur home organist.

Ikutaro Kakehashi ran a television and radio shop in Osaka in the 1950s. He had become fascinated by the idea of electronic musical instruments by way of the theremin and the Ondes Martenot. These instruments seemed to him too difficult for most people to master, so he turned his attention to the electronic organ, having seen one in a local church. He liked the sounds of this small organ so much that he set himself the task of designing and building 'a splendid instrument at a fraction of the price of a traditional pipe organ'.[30]

Leaving his appliance shop to another manager, he founded Ace Electronics in 1960 with the purpose of producing electronic organs. The early organs were designed by Kakehashi and built and marketed by the Technics Corporation. By 1964 the company had begun producing electronic rhythm machines to accompany the home organist, and a few years later began to build their own keyboard instruments.

Kakehashi began developing a machine he called the Rhythm Ace. It used transistors rather than tubes, so was relatively compact and could be mounted below the organ manual. The earlier version did not sell well, but in 1967 he achieved success with the second-generation Rhythm Ace, the FR-1. The Hammond Organ Company began using the units with its organs.

The Song of Roland

A few years later Ace Electronics was taken over by a large Japanese chemical company and, around the same time, Kakehashi began to feel that he could no longer develop his musical ideas with the single-minded Hammond Organ Company. In 1972 he founded a new company, the Roland Corporation, that released three rhythm machines, still focused on the electronic organ market. The most sophisticated of the three was the TR-77 (TR stood for 'transistorized rhythm'). Kakehashi called the unit a rhythm instrument, a prescient notion given the status of his company's drum machines in the history of electronic dance music.

The TR-77 featured about twenty preset rhythm patterns in rock, jazz and Latin styles, two-beat and four-beat switch, and a 'variation' control. Combining the rhythm selector, beat selector and variation knob provided new combinations. Kakehashi had developed a 'diode matrix' to create the various rhythmic patterns. The hard-wired patterns were thus unchangeable, but pushing two rhythm buttons simultaneously provided a composite pattern.

The TR-77's drum sounds (for example, bass drum, conga, bongo) were made from 'tuned resonant' circuits, which consisted of a capacitor, an inductor and a resistor. When receiving a trigger, the circuits resonate or 'ring', producing a percussive sound. Depending on the tuning of the circuit, different drum types could be simulated. The cymbal and hi-hat sounds were created by filtered white noise, and the snare drum sound used both noise and a resonant circuit.

In 1978 Roland released the CR-78 drum machine. It was called the 'Compurhythm' because it contained a microprocessor. While it still contained the Latin, rock and jazz presets, it was the microprocessor that moved the machine away from the home organ market because its memory function allowed the musician to compose, store and replay their own rhythmic patterns.

The English band Ultravox's 1980 hit record 'Vienna' used the CR-78. Drummer Warren Cann describes using the machine:

> At some point before recording 'Vienna' I'd acquired Roland's newest drum machine offering, the infamous 'CR-78' . . . It was still in that awful walnut veneer covered box and still offered

push-button pre-sets for Fox Trots, Sambas, and Tangos. The tempo was set by turning a knob but was still horrendously touchy, if you even looked at it the tempo changed. The sounds were still analog representations. It wasn't all that much better but it did sport a radical new facility; by tapping on a little round rubber pad which you plugged in, you could program your own rhythm into one of four memories. Happening![31]

Blondie's experience with the drum machine was quite transformative in the case of their song 'Heart of Glass'. The CR-78 transformed the way Debbie Harry imagined a song that had been written years before. Not only did they use the sounds and rhythms of the unit, but they utilized the trigger pulse output as a metronome to sync with live drumming on the track.

The drum track of 'In the Air Tonight' by Phil Collins was an integration of his own skills as a drummer and a pattern he found on the machine:

'In the Air Tonight' was just a drum machine pattern that I took off that CR-78 drum machine. You could eliminate certain sounds and program bass drums and snare drums, so I programmed a bass drum part into it, but basically the rest of it was already on there.[32]

The Roland TR-808

Roland released the TR-808 drum machine in 1980, and therein laid the basis for its commercial failure. Whereas the TR-808 relied on analogue circuitry for its drum sounds, its rival drum machine, the Linn LM-1, used digital recordings (samples) for its sounds. The TR-808 was one-fifth the cost of the Linn machine, but just like the TB-303, it received poor reviews for not being 'realistic'-sounding. The TR-808 did not sell well, and by 1984 had become a 'deep discount' item.

The TR-808 was characterized by a rhythmic programming system that was a novel way of imaging rhythm. A series of sixteen buttons, a 'pre-scale' selector and an A/B 'memory mode' allowed for up to thirty-second note subdivisions, triplets, and duple-, triple- and odd-time signatures. The machine was programmed by either a 'tap' method, effectively a 'real-time' programming mode, or a 'step' method where the musician proceeded tick by tick. This visually based system was such that a rhythmic attack point was either on or off, with the 'on' buttons being lit by an LED.

As a percussionist, I was immediately struck by how this representation is remarkably similar in concept to the box notation method developed by musicologist Philip Harland at the University of California in Los Angeles in the early 1960s, known as TUBS (Time Unit Box System). The TUBS representation is popular among ethnomusicologists. The system is effectively a digital representation, with each box being either 'on' or 'off'. The critical difference is that the user does not need to read traditional musical notation, but simply imagines a metric structure (what we call a 'beat' now) and visualizes its subdivisions graphically. While one might imagine that musical rhythmic notation is proportional on the page, it is not. The attack points of notated rhythms are squeezed together to save space on the page of notated music. The 'notation' of the TR-808 was much more accessible to the untrained musician.

One of the most important makers of hip-hop and electro, Afrika Bambaataa, had used a TR-808 to create the drum track on the 1982 hit 'Planet Rock'. There was something about its sound – not realistic, but *futuristic*. And the future in this case was Afro-Futurism, and it was in Detroit.

During the late 1970s Juan Atkins, one of the Belleville Three (along with Derrick May and Kevin Saunderson), was listening to a late-night Detroit radio show hosted by a DJ called The Electrifyin' Mojo. This is where Atkins first heard Kraftwerk, along with George Clinton's Parliament Funkadelic and classic rock: 'Around 1980 I had a tape of nothing but Kraftwerk, Telex, Devo, Giorgio Moroder and Gary Numan, and I'd ride around in my car playing it.'[33] He had learned to mix as a DJ because of the Disco craze, but clearly he was hearing something else in his head.

> During the summer of 1980 I bought myself a Korg MS10 (a small semi-modular voltage-controlled synthesizer). I messed around with that synthesizer all summer, and I'd got to the point where I was making up all sorts of drumbeats on it. I had two Kenwood cassette decks and a little Yamaha four-channel mixer, and I'd make up my drum beat and record it on one deck, then bounce it across onto the other and overdub another part at the same time. I became a real master at doing that; I knew how to EQ [adjusting the balance between frequency ranges in a signal] my drum sounds to start with so that by the time I'd finished four or five overdubs the music still sounded clean.

Joining forces with friend Rick Davis, who had an ARP Odyssey, ARP Axxe, Roland RS09 string machine, the ARP analogue sequencer, a Roland sequencer and a Boss DR-55 Dr Rhythm, they released a record called 'Alleys of Your Mind' in 1981 as Cybotron. The influence of funk and disco was there, but there was something new, something space-age in the form of synthesizers chords and melodies, drum machines and robot voices.

It was Atkins's purchase of a Roland TR-808 drum machine, added to his DJ set-up, that really began to push his music to new places. Atkins claims that he owned

the first 808 in Michigan . . . I had a class called Future
Studies, about the transition from an industrial society to a
technological society. I just applied a lot of those principles to
my music-making . . . The 808 allowed you to actually build
your own patterns – you were able to put the kick drums
and snares where you wanted them. It opened up a lot of
creativity.[34]

In 1985 Atkins released 'No UFOs' on his own label. He
recorded under the name Model 500, not a reference to the
Ford Fairlane 500 model, but something that was, in his mind,
a 'techno/futurist thing'. The record sold 15,000 copies, and DJs
in Detroit, Chicago and Europe were ecstatic.

Sample This

The rise of digital sampling caused the commercial failure of
the TR-808. In my view, the instrumental mimicry provided
by sampling represents, in part, a *confinement* of hearing with
regard to the possibilities of analogue circuitry. Reminiscent of
the public misunderstanding of the synthesizer as a simulation
of acoustic instrumental sounds (clarinet, piano and so on),
sampling began an era of narrowly understood realism. Instead
of circuitry to produce the wonderful, space-age sounds of the
TR-808, the next wave of 'digital' drum machines used short
recordings of actual drum and percussion hits. Each strike was
digitized and contained on its own 'ROM', a fixed computer
storage medium, hence ROM meaning 'read-only memory'.

The first commercially available digital drum machine was
the Linn LM-1. Released in 1980, it was expensive but quickly
became the new drum sound of the decade. It had twelve
sampled drum and percussion sounds and rhythms could be
programmed in individual programming steps (each attack

point of the beat subdivision) or could be played in real time and recorded. It featured two innovations, quantize and swing functions. The quantize function was basically an automatic editing feature that would move the recorded notes to the nearest correct attack point, while the swing function moved the notes into a relationship that simulated a jazz feel to the rhythm. A huge number of musicians used the LM-1, including Prince, Devo, Human League, Kraftwerk, Giorgio Moroder, Jean-Michel Jarre, Vangelis and The Art of Noise. The best-selling album in music history, Michael Jackson's *Thriller*, produced by Quincy Jones, incorporated the LM-1 in the recordings of 'Wanna Be Startin' Somethin', 'Baby, Be Mine', and the title track.

One year later, a second digital drum machine came onto the market. The Oberheim DMX was about two-thirds the cost of Roger Linn's machine. It quickly found its way into hip-hop, synth-pop, new wave and reggae.

In Jamaica Prince Jammy, originally an apprentice at King Tubby's Hometown Hi-Fi Studio, began to produce some of his own records, such as 'Kamikazi dub'. His fame spread when he won the 1985 Big Sound Clash, where several sound systems competed against each other in a 'battle of the bands':

> Jammy won with a single riddim: Under Me Sleng Teng. While the riddim is quite easy the sound of it was outstandingly new – it was produced 100% digital reggae, never heard before at that time! Wayne Smith, a singer for Jammy's, experimented around with a CASIO music box and did some interesting stuff with a slowed down rock 'n' roll preset-drum pattern out of which Tony Asher, keyboardist at Jammy's and one of the few people around who new their ways with the new equipment, build the final riddim. Jammy produced the revolutionary classic of it, which today is one of the most versioned riddims ever.[35]

To create his huge hit 'Under Me Sleng Teng', Jammy (now known as King Jammy) used a Yamaha DX100, Casio CS01 and CZ1000 synthesizers, and an Oberheim DX Drum Machine. The DX was a slightly cut-down version of the DMX, having fewer percussion samples. The Oberheim machine quickly became a staple of dancehall reggae musicians.

Perhaps the most characteristic sound of the DMX would be its underpinning structure on most of the tracks of rap group Run DMC's first album. The song 'Sucker M.C.s' is a rap over nothing but a DMX.

Jazz pianist Herbie Hancock's huge 1983 funk hit 'Rockit' also involved a DMX. Its gut-punching sound on that recording, along with turntables and three synthesizers, arguably restarted Hancock's career.[36] It was a producer who brought Hancock the latest gear for the session, reminiscent of the time when Miles had brought Hancock into the studio for the 1968 'Miles in the Sky' sessions, and instructed him to play an electric piano on one of the tracks. Producer Michael Beinhorn had just purchased a DMX. He laughingly recalls that 'I did the programming, but I didn't know how to program a drum machine, so I had to teach myself.'[37]

Roland's TR-909 drum machine came to the market in 1984. It combined the analogue sound generation of drum sounds with digital samples for its cymbals and hi-hat sounds. It was equipped with MIDI capability, certainly a cutting-edge feature, but soon lost out to the fully 'digital' drum machines of the day. However, no one could have predicted how it and the TR-808 would alter the development of electronic music history when those two antiquated pieces of technology became the heartbeat of the new techno, acid and house genres. We see here a completely unexpected bifurcation between the 'progress' of digital sampling and, at the same time, a recycling and rethinking of analogue technology as a compositional source.

The concept of sampled drum sounds quickly fostered a
new era of 'sampling', but became something even its creator
never imagined. Roger Linn describes how his drum technology
inadvertently generated the next phase of compositional
thought:

> when I made my first drum machines . . . I intended this only
> for drum sounds and didn't offer much memory. I was com-
> pletely blindsided by the idea of people wanting to use them to
> sample entire sections of recordings – loops – and use these as
> elements in a song. As I like to put it, I make the brush and the
> artists choose what to paint with it.[38]

Linn ended up working with Japan's Akai Corporation
to produce the MPC60 Midi Production Center in 1988. It
was a combination of a sampling drum machine and a MIDI
sequencer. Sounds were stored on floppy discs. Since it offered
26 seconds of recording time and could store more than one
hundred samples in its memory, it was really more than just a
drum machine. The sounds could be played by striking rubber
pads on the surface of the machine, or by a MIDI controller such
as a keyboard.

The MPC60 was organized in a 'segment', 'track' and 'song'
format. This format was used on most of the sampler/sequencer
units that came after. A 'segment' could be, for example, a
short repeating drum pattern. A 'track' was like a track on a
multi-track tape recorder. There were 99 tracks and they all
played simultaneously. A 'song' is a list of sequences that play
consecutively, with each sequence representing a phrase or
larger section of a composition. The MPC60 could store up to
twenty songs.

Like the 'box notation' of the TR-808 drum machine, the
segment, track, song format was a simple but brilliant solution

that allowed an untrained musician to, bit by bit – playing it back and listening to it over and over – build up a larger musical form. Josh Davis, known as DJ Shadow, recalls acquiring an MPC60 in 1992:

> I had it expanded as far as it would go . . . I think it was a maximum of five seconds on each pad . . . I did the album [*Endtroducing* . . .] on the MPC-60 MKII, with nothing else, really. It was truly an exploration, as it was with the 4-track. By the time I got the MPC, I was so ready for something new . . . I'd taken the 4-track to the limit, doing everything from putting the tape in on the other side for reverse loops, to everything I could possibly think of . . . I'd fantasized about it for so long that when I got it . . . I stayed up all night reading the manual front to back. I had to use it immediately because I was bursting with all these ideas.[39]

Producer Scott Storch mentions a similar improvisational process when working with rapper Dr Dre where 'he creates a little band. I'll be at the keyboard noodling, and he'll be at the drum machine noodling, and we'll find each other in that way – all of a sudden, boom, there's a record.'[40]

MIDI

MIDI, an acronym for Musical Instrument Digital Interface, was a technological development, but is much more important as a moment when musical ideas – chords, melodies, counterpoint and orchestrations – could be built, connected and synchronized in musical time.

MIDI was the result of a cooperative effect of synthesizer designer Dave Smith and Roland Corporation founder Ikutaro Kakehashi in Japan. Smith's firm, Sequential Circuits, made the first MIDI-equipped synthesizer – the Prophet 600 – in 1982. Within a few years, every manufacturer had adopted the protocol. The MIDI protocol allowed precision control over synthesizers, drum machines, samplers and signal processing units, all from one computer-sequencing program. It was given away free to get manufacturers to encourage them to adopt it – it was an idea that was very much akin to the 'open source' software of the present era. Dave Smith recalls the pre-MIDI world:

> You could play one keyboard with your right hand and another keyboard with your left hand. But [musicians] couldn't play more than one at the same time because there was no way of electrically interconnecting them.[41]

Think of MIDI data as a player-piano roll, except that instead of buying it and just playing back pre-punched piano music, the musician could now record their own 'roll' directly. When connected with a cable, MIDI protocol can send and receive up to sixteen channels of data. Each chunk of data carries the information about a single note event, that is, its pitch, loudness and control signals such as vibrato and stereo panning. It does not transmit sound, but instead a real-time 'score' to be played by the synthesizer or drum machine. It also carries a MIDI clock pulse that allows for the timing and synchronization of multiple devices such as synthesizers, drum machines, samples, effects and processing units, computers and controllers such as a keyboard or other MIDI instrument such as a MIDI-equipped guitar. Individual MIDI channels are conceptually similar to a multi-track tape recorder, so each channel could be connected to a single synthesizer or drum machine. MIDI data can also be recorded into a hardware or software device, usually a sequencer or a

DAW (Digital Audio Workstation). The data is fully portable and editable – just like word processing – and does not require much computer memory.

Dave Stewart of the Eurythmics gives a sense of the power of MIDI:

> One day I was going past a music store in Camden Town and there was a crowd inside so I went in and there was a kind of hush whilst someone was explaining that this Sequential Circuits Prophet 600 had MIDI! Once I grasped what they were talking about I felt quite faint, my head spinning with the possibilities. I've never been the same since and neither has the rest of the world.[42]

MIDI was yet another step in the drastic changes around the accessibility of electronic musical instruments. It didn't require knowledge of written music, just the burgeoning computer skills that young generations were absorbing quickly. A computer-sequencing program for MIDI composition is completely visual, with the rhythmic and metric grid laid out vertically and associated pitch levels displayed horizontally. Changes and additions can be easily edited using delete, copy and paste and so on, just like a word-processing program. Again, this was a completely liberating user interface for all levels of musicians doing electronic music. The Orb's Alex Paterson praised it exuberantly:

> God bless MIDI . . . Everybody could join in . . . It was like walking into a dream . . . you could be playing something on one synth and then you could walk over to the next synth and you could be playing the exact same thing. It was all there stored up ready to go . . .[43]

MIDI controllers completely revolutionized the way we could perform and compose music. The first basic MIDI controller was a traditional keyboard, usually with two 'wheels' that could be rocked forward and backward. One usually, detented in at its midpoint, would 'bend' the keyed pitch up or down with a slide or portamento. The other could be 'assigned' (programmed) to act upon some other effect, for example, vibrato or a filter setting. The next wave of controllers used pitch-to-MIDI convertors to automatically code input from purpose-built acoustic instruments and microphones in real time.

In recent years, MIDI controllers have been available in a plentiful array of both custom-made and commercially available devices. Musicians now use traditional keyboards, tabletop drum pads, electronic drum sets, human breath controllers, light and motion sensing devices, game controllers, foot pedals and even accordions and theremins.

Electronic composer/performer Holly Herndon discusses this new way of musical thinking:

> I use a MIDI controller when I perform live and also when I'm writing ... Maybe this kind of Western piano interface isn't the best way to write music. And that's what's so interesting about MIDI, maybe the best way to compose a piece is to turn a knob in a certain way or to use faders. And that's, I think, you know, not to overblow it, but that's really kind of revolutionized the way we approach composition.[44]

The development of MIDI created the possibility of a powerful, relatively affordable 'home studio'. From children to adults, amateurs to professionals, these 'bedroom composers', as they are sometimes called, are making music, and playing the roles of composers, performers and recording engineers.

Electronic Dance Music (EDM) has really flourished as a genre because of MIDI technology. The shift that the DJ made from just playing music to being a composer/producer of music was critical in fostering a generation of individual composers who are able to work alone in ad hoc home studios by taking advantage of the new interconnectability of their equipment. Tom Jenkinson, known professionally as Squarepusher, is a good example of this new kind of one-person band:

> I just like the idea, the thing of getting out of bed, going and getting your breakfast, then come back and you're straight in the studio. You don't have to go down the road and get on a bus to go to the studio . . . it's hands-on straight away.[45]

As MIDI technology facilitated a range of EDM genres, many artists continued to use analogue equipment and began to blend synthesis, sampling and drum machines using MIDI control. Squarepusher, discussing his 1997 EP 'Big Loada', notes that:

> I made my first records using the Boss DR660, which was a bit of a non-event in the history of drum machines. It just happened to be the one I could afford at the time and that had a reasonable range of sounds on it and that could do MIDI sequencing. But it was phenomenally limited. To this day, nobody believes that the tracks on 'Big Loada' were a single pass of me sequencing my Akai S950 [sampler] from my DR660.[46]

As we have seen in numerous other occasions in this book, there is rarely a complete or immediate shift to new technologies. Rather, composers are always finding different configurations of hardware and software – old and new – to make their work. However, in recent years two software engines have been taken up by a variety of composers and sound artists.

Ableton Live is software that combines audio and MIDI sequencing, editing and processing. In addition to being a tool for composing and recording, its real power lies in its use as a real-time musical instrument. With transport controls like a tape recorder, Live counts time within a standard musical grid – time signature, beats, measures and tempo – but allows the user to 'drag and drop' audio files into the running 'set', as it is called. The program automatically 'beat-matches' and loops the segments, which can be sequenced, turned on and off, copied, deleted, replaced and so on seamlessly – all 'without missing a beat'.

The musically transformative power of Ableton Live is evidenced by the wide range of artists embracing it. Trombonist and AACM composer/improviser George Lewis recalls his experience as he began to move away from his primary instrument while working with the German electronic musicians Sigi Rössert and Ulrich Müller:

> I have always had a real ambivalence about the trombone. It got acute after I had some real success as a trombone player, and then it was like, Well, if you don't play the trombone you're worthless, you know? As a creative artist I thought, I didn't sign up for this, to have a brass albatross around my neck (laughter). Electronics were the road out of that, and there I am with Sigi and Ulrich, and I'm thinking, Well, I could be doing more of this. This is what I'm interested in, creating sound in real time and improvising with them, and they're all using this Ableton Live software. They showed me how it worked and I started using it . . .[47]

MIT Media Lab member Miller Puckette began developing a program called MAX for the MacIntosh personal computer in

1987. Released commercially by Opcode Systems in 1990, it was an immediate success, finding its way to many different kinds of musicians and composers. Named after computer music pioneer Max Mathews, the first version offered a whole new look at the possibilities of MIDI composition, particularly the area of live performance. Previous sequencing software focused on the recording and editing of sequences, song sections and MIDI orchestration. While MAX offered such possibilities it was, in the words of Miller Puckette, 'oriented toward processes more than data. (There is no built-in notion of a musical "score," for example.) If we think of a Max patch as a collection of boxes interconnected by lines, the expressiveness of Max comes from its interconnection and intercommunication facilities . . .'[48]

As an interface with hardware synthesizers, drum machines and outboard effects processors, Max extended the power of MIDI by offering a whole range of organizing musical events. These included powerful mathematical tools, logical decision-making, probability and randomization of musical events. Additionally, its ability to both send and receive MIDI data made it truly interactive.

In 1997 Puckette added a large set of objects that offered the possibility of creating and manipulating digital audio signals in real time. For the first time, many of the original mainframe synthesis techniques could be used on the fly on a laptop computer. Named MSP (MAX Signal Processing), this development was followed a few years later by the addition of 'Jitter objects', designed to create and manipulate digital video images.

Pauline Oliveros began developing her Expanded Instrument System (EIS) in 1965. Beginning as a live tape-delay system, it has undergone many changes with the advent of music technology and is now a MAX/MSP package. Oliveros describes the design:

Acoustic input from an instrument or voice now can be
processed with up to forty variable delays, modulated with
fluctuating waveforms, layered and spatialized. Sounds may
be diffused in four, six or eight channels. More outputs could
be programmed for sixteen, thirty-two, sixty-four and beyond
. . . Even though the idea derived from echo is very simple the
applications of digital signal processing and routing result
in endless variations and possibilities. The current revision
of the patch also includes some intelligent controls for the
innumerable parameters involved. These controllers can learn
from experience. The controls can be set to run from a chaos
generator or from a random event generator as well.[49]

MAX/MSP has been incorporated into the Ableton Live
program. MAX for Live provides a virtual instrument inside
the looping program. This amalgam was the result of a 'chance
meeting' between the creators of the programs when Live was
first released:

Ableton's Robert Henke commented to Cycling 74's David
Zicarelli that what Live needed was a similar versatility:
a special 'edit button' to allow built-in effects to be altered and
modified directly without stopping the music. The idea behind
Max For Live was born, and nearly a decade later, the technology has been developed to actually make it work.[50]

Norwegian nu-jazz guitarist Eivind Aarset is rarely
photographed without a laptop in front of him. Aarset uses
Ableton Live both for creating and processing loops. Blending
live performance with beats and samples, his music would not
really be feasible without this addition to his electric guitar and
effects units.

I use Live for reworking loops and for more extreme processing of my guitars . . . You can put in any sound, process it and get serious changes in a way that is very appealing to me . . . But perhaps the strongest attribute of Live is its ability to create rhythmically interesting riffs and grooves. I find that by moving the Warp Makers around in the Clip View and working with pitch at the same time, thereby changing the accents, I can actually create a total change of the feel and characteristics of the riff or loop tonally, sonically, and rhythmically.[51]

While programs like MAX/MSP and Ableton Live have, in many ways, encapsulated the enormous variety of electronic music practices from tape manipulation techniques, to modulation synthesis, to scratching and sampling, their real value may lie in their capacity to be shaped and molded by musicians and composers across many musical genres and outward from the virtual space of the computers they inhabit.

Computer music making today may be the example, par excellence, of the eversion (turning inside out) of an imagined 'cyberspace' – whether through the use of midi and game controllers, Arduino boards, body sensors, contact mics or live sound input – to, as theorist N. Katherine Hayles describes, 'environments in which physical and virtual realms merge in fluid and seamless ways.'[52] As these musical systems evolve, with digital data and media brought into direct contact with physical objects, in physical space, the computer as a musical instrument will continue to flourish.

EPILOGUE

When Robert Fripp disbanded King Crimson in 1974, he described a 'new world: small, mobile, independent, and intelligent units . . . instead of a city, you'll get small self-sufficient communities, modern villages. And instead of King Crimson, you're now getting me – a small, independent, mobile, and intelligent unit.'[1] This was a particularly prescient notion. With music technology constantly becoming more portable, more affordable and more hackable (for example, Arduino boards and open-source music software), we are really seeing, in a broad sense, exactly what Fripp described.

Writing on laptop music in Japan, Emmanuelle Loube described 'the emergence of a new concept of the "artist"', a concept that is, I believe, applicable everywhere:

> It is a culture of emergence: a non-directional, non-intentional culture that leaves much room for error and blur. It is a culture that encourages 'averageness' over creativity, but it has the advantage of provoking unexpected results.[2]

In a very real sense, we now live in a world of micro-electronic music cultures, much in the spirit of Marcel Duchamp, who advocated that the artist go 'underground'. He worked secretly for twenty years on his final work, *Étant Donnés: 1e la chute d'eau, 2e le gaz d'éclairage* (Given: 1. The Waterfall, 2. The Illuminating Gas), a proto-installation constructed in a studio on West 11th Street in New York City. These emergent, independent, ad hoc, microelectronic music cultures are also very much in the spirit of the utopian premise – and promise – of the early days of electronic music: *any sound is possible.*

RECOMMENDED LISTENING

808 State	*Newbuild* (1998)
Amacher, Maryanne	*Living Sound* (1979)
AMM Ensemble	*Live Electronic Music Improvised* (1968)
Anderson, Laurie	*Big Science* (1982)
Anderson, Ruth	*Points* (1974)
Aphex Twin	*Selected Ambient Works* (1985–92)
Arel, Bülent	*Stereo Electronic Music No. 1* (1960)
Arfib, Daniel	*Le Souffle du Doux* (1979)
Art of Noise	*Beat Box (Diversion One)* (1984)
Ashley, Robert	*The Wolfman* (1964)
	She Was a Visitor (1979)
Atkins, Juan	*20 Years* (1985–2005)
Autechre	*Incunabula* (1993)
	LP5 (1998)
Babbitt, Milton	*Composition for Synthesizer* (1961)
	Ensembles for Synthesizer (1963)
	Philomel (1964)
	Phonemena (1974)
Bambaataa, Afrika	*Planet Rock* (1986)
Barrier, Jean-Baptiste	*Chreode I* (1983)
Barron, Bebe and Louis	Soundtrack for *Forbidden Planet* (1956)
Basinski, William	*The Disintegration Loops* (2002–3)
Beatles, the	*Magical Mystery Tour* (1967)
	White Album (1968)
Beaver, Paul, and Bernie Krause	*The Nonesuch Guide to Electronic Music* (1968)
Behrman, David	*Wave Train* (1966)
	Runthrough (1967)
	On the Other Ocean (1978)

Berio, Luciano	*Thema: Omaggio a Joyce* (1958)
	Différences (1960)
	Visage (1961)
Bley, Paul	*Revenge* (with Annette Peacock) (1969)
	Scorpio (1973)
Boulez, Pierre	*Répons* (1981)
Braxton, Anthony	*Composition No. 107* (1982)
Brun, Herbert	*Dust* (1976)
	i toLD You so (1981)
Bryars, Gavin	*1, 2, 1–2–3–4* (1971)
Byrd, Joseph	*American Metaphysical Circus* (1968)
Cage, John	*Imaginary Landscape No. 1* (1939)
	Williams Mix (1952)
	Fontana Mix (1959)
Can	*Father Cannot Yell* (1969)
	Tago Mago (1971)
Carlos, Wendy	*Switched on Bach* (1968)
	Timesteps (1972)
Cascone, Kim	*1parasitefordeleuze* (2000)
Chadabe, Joel	*Modalities* (1989)
Choi, Insook	*Later, the Runaway, Leaving No Trace, Not Even a Trace of Misfortune* (1991)
Chowning, John	*Stria* (1977)
	Phoné (1981)
Cluster	*Cluster 71* (1971)
	Cluster/Eno (1977)
Davidovsky, Mario	*Synchronisms Nos. 1–12* (1963–2006)
Davis, Miles	*In a Silent Way* (1969)
	Bitches Brew (1970)
	Live-evil (1970)
	On the Corner (1972)
Derbyshire, Delia	*Dreams* (1964)
	Electrosonic (1972)
Dhomont, Francis	*et autres utopies* (2006)
	Forêt Profonde (1996)
DJ Spooky	*Optometry* (2002)
Dockstader, Tod	*Apocalypse II* (1961)
Dodge, Charles	*The Earth's Magnetic Field* (1970)
	Synthesized Voices (1976)
Dunn, David	*Four Electroacoustic Compositions* (2002)

Eimert, Herbert, and Robert Beyer	*Klangstudie II* (1952)
Emerson, Lake, and Palmer	*Emerson, Lake, and Palmer* (1970)
Eno, Brian	*No Pussyfooting* (with Robert Fripp) (1972)
	Discreet Music (1975)
	Ambient 1/Music for Airports (1978)
Fast, Larry	*Sequencer* (1976)
Fennesz, Christian	*Hotel Paral.lel* (1997)
	Endless Summer (2001)
Ferrari, Luc	*Études aux accidents* (1958)
	Études aux son tendus (1958)
	J'ai été coupé (1969)
	Presque rien (1970)
	Presque rien No. 2 (1977)
	Presque rien avec filles (1989)
	Presque rien No. 4 (1998)
Fontana, Bill	*Soundbridge Köln/San Francisco* (1987)
Galás, Diamanda	*You Must Be Certain of the Devil* (1988)
Goldie	*Timeless* (1995)
Grandmaster Flash	'The Adventures of Grandmaster Flash on the Wheels of Steel' (1982)
Gressel, Joel	*Points in Time* (1974)
Günter, Bernhard	*Un peu de neige salie* (1993)
Hancock, Herbie	*Sextant* (1973)
	Rockit (1983)
Harvey, Jonathan	*Mortuos Plango, Vivos Voco* (1980)
Henry, Pierre	*Le microphone bien temperé* (1951)
	Variations pour une porte et un soupir (1963)
	L'Apocalypse de Jean (1968)
Herndon, Holly	*Movement* (2012)
	Platform (2015)
Hiller, Lejaren	*Illiac Suite* (1957)
	HPSCHD w/ *John Cage* (1969)
Ichiyanagi, Toshi	*Extended Voices* (1967)
Inoue, Tetsu	*Psycho-acoustic* (1998)
Jeck, Philip	*Vinyl Coda I–IV* (2000–2001)
Kid 606	PS *I Love You* (2000)
King Jammy	*Under Me Sleng Teng* (1985)
King Tubby	*Termination Dub* (1973–9)
	Dangerous Dub (1981)

Köner, Thomas	*Permafrost* (1993)
Kraftwerk	*Autobahn* (1974)
	Radio-activity (1975)
	Trans-Europe Express (1977)
Lansky, Paul	*Six Fantasies on a Poem of Thomas Campion* (1979)
	Idle Chatter (1985)
	Notjustmoreidlechatter (1990)
Le Caine, Hugh	*Dripsody* (1955)
Leedy, Douglas	*Entropical Paradise* (1968)
Lewis, George	*Voyager: Improvised Duos between Human and Computer*
	Musicians (1993)
Ligeti, Györgi	*Glissandi* (1957)
	Artikulation (1958)
Lockwood Annea	*World Rhythms* (1975)
	A Sound Map of the Hudson River (2003)
Lopez, Francisco	*La Selva* (1998)
	Wind [Patagonia] (2007)
LTJ Bukem	*Logical Progression* (1996)
Lucier, Alvin	*Music for Solo Performer* (1965)
	North American Time Capsule (1967)
	I am Sitting in a Room (1970)
	Music on a Long, Thin Wire (1979)
Luening, Otto	*Low Speed* (1952)
McNabb, Michael	*Dreamsong* (1984)
Marclay, Christian	*Record Without a Cover* (1985)
	Records (1997)
	Ghost [I Don't Live Today] (2007)
Matching Mole	*Matching Mole* (1972)
Maxfield, Richard	*Sine Music: A Swarm of Butterflies Over the Ocean* (1959)
Meat Beat Manifesto	*Actual Sounds + Voices* (1998)
Merzbow	*Merzbox Sampler* (1998)
Messiaen, Olivier	*Oraison* (1937)
Mimaroglu, Ílhan	*Preludes for Magnetic Tape* (1966–7)
MIMEO	*Electric Chair + Table* (2000)
Mouse on Mars	*Iaora Tahiti* (1995)
Mumma, Gordon	*Hornpipe* (1967)
	Electronic Music of Theatre and Public Activity (2005)

Musica Elettronica Viva	*Spacecraft* (1967)
	Sound Pool (1969)
	MEV 40 (1967–2007)
Neuhaus, Max	*Electronics and Percussion* (1968)
	Radio Net (1977)
	Times Square (1977–92)
New Order	*Substance* (1987)
Nono, Luigi	*Como una ola fuerza y luz* (1972)
	. . . Sofferte onde serene (1979)
	Complete Works for Solo Tape (1960–74)
Oldfield, Mike	*Tubular Bells* (1973)
	Hergest Ridge (1974)
Oliveros, Pauline	*Bye Bye Butterfly* (1965)
	I of IV (1966)
	Alien Bog (1967)
Oneohtrix Point Never	*Returnal* (2010)
	Replica (2011)
Oram, Daphne	*Electronic Sound Patterns* (1962)
Orbital	*Orbital* (1991)
Oswald, John	*69 Plunderphonics 96* (1996)
Oval	*Systemisch* (1994)
Pan Sonic	*Vakio* (1995)
	Kulma (1997)
Parmegiani, Bernard	*Pop'eclectic* (1973)
	La Crèation du monde (1984)
	De Natura Sonorum (2000)
Payne, Maggi	*Resonant Places* (1992)
Peacock, Annette	*1/2 Broken* (1983)
Perry, Lee 'Scratch'	*Ultimate Collection* (1970–79)
Phuture	*Acid Trax* (1987)
Pink Floyd	*Dark Side of the Moon* (1973)
Pousseur, Henry	*Scambi* (1957)
	Trois visages de Liège (1961)
Randall, J. K.	*Mudgett: Monologues by a Mass Murderer* (1965)
	Lyric Variations (1968)
	Quartersines (1969)
Reed, Lou	*Metal Machine Music* (1975)
Reich, Steve	*It's Gonna Rain* (1965)
	Come Out (1966)

	Violin Phase (1967)
	Pendulum Music (1968)
Riley, Terry	*A Rainbow in Curved Air* (1969)
Risset, Jean Claude	*Mutations* (1969)
	L'Autre face (1983)
	Sud (1984)
Roads, Curt	*nscor* (1980)
Rockmore, Clara	*Valse Sentimentale (Tchaikovsky)* (1977)
Rosenboom, David	*Systems of Judgment* (1989)
Saariaho, Kaija	*Petals* (1988)
Sauders, Jesse	*On and On* (1984)
Scaletti, Carla	*sunSurgeAutomata* (1987)
Schaeffer, Pierre	*Cinq études de bruits* (1948)
	Symphonie pour un homme seul (1950)
	Étude aux objets (1967)
Schafer, R. Murray	*The Vancouver Soundscape* (1973)
Semegen, Daria	*Electronic Composition No. 1* (1971)
Shields, Alice	*Study for Voice and Tape* (1968)
	The Transformation of Ani (1970)
Size, Roni	*New Forms* (1997)
Smalley, Denis	*Wind Chimes* (1987)
Smiley, Pril	*Kolyosa* (1970)
Spiegel, Laurie	*Appalachian Grove* (1974)
Squarepusher	*Big Loada* (1997)
Stockhausen, Karlheinz	*Konkrete Etüde* (1952)
	Studie I (1953)
	Studie II (1954)
	Gesang der Jünglinge (1956)
	Kontakte (1960)
	Mikrophonie I (1964)
	Telemusik (1966)
	Hymnen (1967)
	Kurzwellen (1968)
	Mantra (1970)
Subotnik, Morton	*Silver Apples of the Moon* (1967)
	The Wild Bull (1968)
Sun Ra	*My Brother the Wind* (1970)
Takemitsu, Toru	*Water Music* (1960)
Tangerine Dream	*Electronic Meditation* (1969)
	Alpha Centauri (1971)
	Zeit (1972)

	Atem (1973)
	Phaedra (1974)
	Rubicon (1975)
	Richochet (1975)
Tenney, James	*Analogue #1: Noise Study* (1961)
	Collage No. 1 'Blue Suede' (1961)
Tomita, Isao	*Snowflakes are Dancing* (1974)
Tonto's Expanding Head Band	*Zero Time* (1971)
Tortoise	*Millions Now Living Will Never Die* (1996)
Truax, Barry	*Arras* (1980)
Tudor, David	*Rainforest Version 1* (1968)
Ussachevsky, Vladimir	*Sonic Contours* (1952)
	Wireless Fantasy (1960)
Varèse, Edgard	*Poème électronique* (1958)
Watson, Chris	*Outside the Circle of Fire* (1998)
Weather Report	*Weather Report* (1971)
	Black Market (1976)
Westerkamp, Hildegard	*Transformations* (1996)
Wishart, Trevor	*Vox Cycle* (1980–88)
Wright, Maurice	*Electronic Composition* (1973)
Xenakis, Iannis	*Diamorphoses II* (1957)
	Concrete PH (1958)
	Orient-Occident III (1960)
	Bohor I (1962)
	Hibiki-Hana-Ma (1970)
	Mycenae-Alpha (1978)
	Voyage absolu des Unari vers Andromede (1989)
Zappa, Frank	*Uncle Meat* (1969)

REFERENCES

Introduction

1 Walter Benjamin, 'The Work of Art in the Age of Mechanical Reproduction', in *Illuminations* (New York, 1968), pp. 217–51.
2 See my *Audio Culture: Readings in Modern Music*, ed. with Christoph Cox (New York, 2004).
3 Jacques Attali, *Noise: The Political Economy of Music* (Minneapolis, MT, 1985), p. 4.
4 Entry on 'Indeterminacy' in *Dictionary of Contemporary Music*, ed. John Vinton (New York, 1971), p. 336. Some further discussion is needed here. Note that Childs says a collection of sound events doesn't necessarily have to be hierarchical, but it can be. Likewise, any means of generating sounds includes indeterminacy, improvisation or highly structured composition.
5 Deke Dickerson, 'Scotty Moore's Royal Legacy: Bearing Witness at the Birth of Rock and Roll', www.guitarplayer.com (29 June 2016).
6 Zofia Lissa, Eugenia Tanska and Eugenia Tarska, 'On the Evolution of Musical Perception', *Journal of Aesthetics and Art Criticism*, XXIV/2 (Winter 1965), p. 274.
7 Ola Stockfelt, 'Adequate Modes of Listening', in *Keeping Score: Music, Disciplinarity, Culture* (Charlottesville, VA, 1997), pp. 132, 137.

1 Tape Recorder

1 See my *Audio Culture: Readings in Modern Music* (New York, 2004).
2 William J. Mitchell, *The Reconfigured Eye* (Cambridge, MA, 1992), p. 3.
3 BASF Corporation, '1925–1944: New Forms of High-pressure Synthesis', www.basf.com, 2014.

4   Freidrich Engel, 'Walter Weber's Technical Innovations at the Reichs-Rundfunk-Gesellschaft', www.richardhess.com, 2006.

5   Jack Mullin, 'Discovering Magnetic Tape', *Broadcast Engineering*, XXI (1979), p. 81.

6   Otto Luening, 'An Unfinished History of Electronic Music', *Music Educators Journal*, LV/3 (November 1968), pp. 45–6.

7   Pierre Schaeffer, *In Search of a Concrete Music*, trans. Christine North and John Dack (Berkeley, CA, 2012), p. 7.

8   Ibid., pp. 7–8.

9   Ibid., p. 14.

10 Ibid., p. 47.

11 Edgard Varèse and Chou Wen-chung, 'The Liberation of Sound', *Perspectives of New Music*, V/1 (1966), p. 11.

12 Interview by Dan Warburton, 22 July 1998, liner notes, Nonesuch recording h-71246.

13 Luc Ferrari, www.paristransatlantic.com, 1998.

14 Ibid.

15 Bill Hopkins, 'Stockhausen and Others', *Tempo*, New Series, XCVIII (1972), p. 34.

16 Roger Smalley, Review of 'Avant-garde 3', *Musical Times*, CXII/1540 (June 1971), p. 567. Smalley does not even mention *Presque rien*, saving his vitriol for the other Ferrari piece on the disc *Société II*, calling it 'crude' and 'gasping at the starting line'.

17 Luc Ferrari in Michel Chion and Guy Reibel, *Les musiques électroacoustiques* (Paris, 1976), p. 66.

18 John Cage, *Imaginary Landscape No. 5* (New York, 1951), p. 2.

19 Ralph Hartsock and Carl Rahkonen, *Vladimir Ussachevsky: A Bio-bibliography* (Westport, CT, 2000), pp. 10–11.

20 Jacques Poullin, 'The Application of Recording Techniques to the Production of New Musical Materials and Forms Applications to Musique Concrète', trans. D. A. Sinclair (Ottawa, 1957), p. 17.

21 Chamberlin also developed a drum machine.

22 George Martin, 'Mellotron', www.theanalogues.net, 2016.

23 Michael King, *Wrong Movements: A Robert Wyatt History* (Wembley, 1994), n.p.

24 Ibid.

25 William S. Marles, 'Duration and Frequency Alteration', *Journal of the Audio Engineering Society*, XIV/2 (1966), p. 133.

26 Pitch modulation effects were apparently possible as well.

27 Reverberation is created by a series of sound reflections but they are fast enough to be perceived as one sound event. An echo

results from a slower sound reflection, thus being perceived as a separate, new sound event.

28 Hartsock and Rahkonen, *Vladimir Ussachevsky*, p. 7.

29 Chick Corea,'Anecdotes: The Man, the Myth, the Legends', www.fenderrhodes.com, 2016.

30 Theodor Adorno, 'On Popular Music', in *Essays on Music*, trans. Susan H. Gillespie (Berkeley, CA, 2002), p. 458.

31 St Augustine, *Confessions*, Book 10, available at www.gutenberg.org. My friend Peter Stallybrass once summarized this quote as 'When I repeat, I do not repeat.'

32 Wikipedia entry on 'Repetition', https://en.wikipedia.org, accessed 2015.

33 Gabrielle Zuckerman, 'An Interview with Steve Reich', *American Public Media*, 2002.

34 Eddie Kramer, 'Jimi Hendrix: Phasing Playback', www.eddie-kramer.com, 2016.

35 Brian Eno, 'Evolving Metaphors, in My Opinion, Is What Artists Do,' www.inmotionmagazine.com, 1996.

36 Rob Tannenbaum, 'A Meeting of Sound Minds: John Cage and Brian Eno', *Musician*, LXXXIII (September 1985), p. 68.

37 Michael Nyman, *Experimental Music: Cage and Beyond* (New York, 1974), p. 75.

38 Gavin Bryars, liner notes on *Ensemble Pieces* (Obscure Records No. 2, 1975).

39 Quoted in Ben Watson, *Frank Zappa: The Negative Dialectics of Poodle Play* (New York, 1995), p. 23.

40 Frank Zappa, liner notes for *Uncle Meat* (Bizarre/Reprise 2MS 2024).

41 George Martin with Jeremy Hornsby, *All You Need is Ears* (New York, 1979), pp. 200–201.

42 Ibid., p. 205.

43 Don Heckman, 'Jazz-rock', *Stereo Review*, XXXIII/5 (1974), p. 75.

44 Teo Macero, 'In a Silent Way', http://journalofmusic.com, 2015.

45 Ibid.

46 Ibid.

47 Frank Ogden and Ray Carter, 'The Country Life', *Studio Sound* (October 1976), p. 38.

48 Richard Newman, *The Making of Mike Oldfield's Tubular Bells* (Cambridge, 1993), p. 57.

49 Bernard Benoliel, 'Oldfield: With and Without Bedford', *Tempo*, New Series, CXX (March 1977), p. 28.

50 Ogden and Carter, 'The Country Life', p. 38.

2 Circuits

1 Edgard Varèse and Chou Wen-Chung, 'The Liberation of Sound', *Perspectives of New Music*, V/1 (Autumn–Winter 1966), p. 18.
2 Richard Kostelanetz, 'John Cage and Richard Kostelanetz: A Conversation About Radio', *Musical Quarterly*, LXXII/2 (1986), p. 218.
3 Anaïs Nin, *The Diary of Anaïs Nin*, vol. VI (New York, 2012), pp. 51–2.
4 Ibid.
5 Ibid.
6 See Richard Toop, 'Stockhausen and the Sine-wave: The Story of an Ambiguous Relationship', *Musical Quarterly*, LXV/3 (1979).
7 Ibid., p. 388.
8 Herbert Eimert, 'Electronic Music', trans. D. A. Sinclair (Ottawa, 1954), p. 3.
9 That same year at the Brussels World's Fair, Varèse's *Poème Electronique* featured the spatial movement of his piece around the Philips Pavilion through 480 speakers.
10 Trevor Pinch and Frank Trocco, *Analog Days: The Invention and Impact of the Moog Synthesizer* (Cambridge, MA, 2002), p. 39.
11 Keith Emerson, *The Art of Electronic Music*, ed. Greg Armbruster (New York, 1984), pp. 142–3.
12 Kenneth Ansell, 'Annette Peacock', *Impetus*, VIII (1978), p. 326.
13 Ibid.
14 Donald Buchla, 'Buchla Synthesizers 1966', http://120years.net, accessed 2016.
15 Morton Subotnick, ibid.
16 David Bernstein, ed., *The San Francisco Tape Music Center* (Berkeley, CA, 2008), pp. 90–91.
17 Pauline Oliveros, 'Some Sound Observations', in *Audio Culture: Readings in Modern Music* (New York, 2004), p. 106.
18 Pauline Oliveros, 'Alien Bog – Beautiful Scoop', www.pogus.com, accessed 2016.
19 Douglas Leedy, Liner notes to *Entropical Paradise*, Seraphim SIC-6060.
20 Private communication with Todd Barton, 2016.
21 Mick Wall, 'The Keys to My Success: Jean Michel Jarre', www.dailymail.co.uk, 2008.
22 Joe Zawinul, 'Zawinul's Keyboards', www.zawinulonline.org, 2015.
23 Ibid.
24 Éliane Radigue, 'The Mysterious Power of the Infinitesimal', *Leonardo Music Journal*, XIX (2009), pp. 48–9.

25 Mark Prendergast, 'Tangerine Dream: Changing Use of Technology, Part 1: 1967–1977', *Sound on Sound* (December 1994), p. 6.

26 Giorgio Moroder, 'How We Made "I Feel Love"', https://noisey.vice.com, 2014.

27 Herbie Hancock, 'Creating Future2Future and Touring in Surround', www.soundonsound.com, 2002.

28 Bob Gluck, *The Miles Davis Lost Quintet and Other Revolutionary Ensembles* (Chicago, IL, 2016), p. 98.

29 Allen Strange referred to the self-generating patch this way in his book *Electronic Music: Synthesis, Techniques, Controls* (Dubuque, IA, 1983), p. 85.

30 Stuart Bennet, *A History of Control Engineering, 1800–1930* (London, 1986), p. 18.

31 Ibid., p. 189.

32 David Sheff, *All We are Saying* (New York, 2000), p. 173.

33 Barry Miles, *Paul McCartney: Many Years From Now* (New York, 1997), p. 172.

34 Arnie Passman, 'Such Sweet Thunder: Charlie Butten and His Earthy Sound System', *Rolling Stone*, XC (1971), p. 38.

35 Ibid.

36 Lou Reed, quoted in David Fricke's liner notes on *Metal Machine Music*, Buddha Records CD 74465 99752 2.

37 Lester Bangs, *Psychotic Reactions and Carburetor Dung* (New York, 1987), p. 200.

3 Turntable and Record

1 Richard Kostelanetz, 'John Cage and Richard Kostelanetz: A Conversation about Radio', *Musical Quarterly*, LXXII/2 (1986), p. 216.

2 Ibid., p. 218.

3 Pierre Schaeffer, *In Search of a Concrete Music*, trans. Christine North and John Dack (Berkeley, CA, 2012), pp. 14–15.

4 Davey D, 'Interview with DJ Kool Herc', www.daveyd.com, 1989.

5 Matthew Bennett, 'Dubplate Culture: Analogue Islands in the Digital Stream', http://daily.redbullmusicacademy.com, 2014.

6 Miles White, 'The Phonograph Turntable and Performance Practice in Hip Hop Music', *Ethnomusicology OnLine* 2 (1996), retrieved 4 February 2013.

7 Ibid.

8 Ibid.

9   David Albert Mhadi Goldberg, 'The Scratch is Hip-hop:
     Appropriating the Phonographic Medium', in *Appropriating
     Technology: Vernacular Science and Social Power* (Minneapolis, MN,
     2004), p. 107.

10 Richard Shusterman, 'The Fine Art of Rap', *New Literary History*,
     XXII/3 (Summer 1991), p. 614.

11 Jacques Attali, *Noise: The Political Economy of Music*, trans. Brian
     Masumi (Minneapolis, MN, 1985), p. 3.

12 Grandmaster Flash with David Ritz, *The Adventures of Grandmaster
     Flash: My Life, My Beats* (New York, 2008), p. 150.

13 See John Oswald's 'Plunderphonics or Audio Piracy as a
     Compositional Prerogative', www.plunderphonics.com.

14 Christian Marclay, Liner notes to *Records, 1981–1989*, Atavistic
     Records alp62cd.

15 Ibid.

16 Philip Jeck, 'Ghosts in the Speakers: Interview with Philip Jeck',
     www.unprojects.org.au, accessed 2016.

17 Ibid.

18 Glenn Gould, 'The Prospects of Recording', *High Fidelity Magazine*,
     16 (1966), p. 341.

19 Glenn Gould, 'Turning His Back on the Audience',
     www.laphamsquarterly.org, 2017.

20 Michael Lydon, *Boogie Lightning: How Music Became Electric*
     (New York, 1980). I am indebted to Jeremy Wallach, whose article
     'The Poetics of Electrosonic Presence: Recorded Music and The
     Materiality of Sound', *Journal of Popular Music Studies* (2003),
     pp. 34–64, brought me to Lydon's book and deepened my thinking
     about the materiality of the vinyl record.

21 Ibid., p. 41.

22 Ibid., p. 42.

23 Ibid., p. 43.

24 Roland Barthes, 'The Grain of the Voice', in *Image-Music-Text*, trans.
     Stephen Heath (London, 1977).

25 John Durham Peters, 'Helmholtz, Edison, and Sound Theory', in
     Memory Bytes: History, Technology, and Digital Culture, ed. Laren
     Rabinovitz and Abraham Geil (Durham, NC, 2004), p. 184.

26 Ibid.

27 Björn Hellström, 'Modelling of Sound in Public Spaces'
     (Stockholm, 2001).

28 Lydon, *Boogie Lightning*, p. 39.

4 Microphone

1 Michael Bakan, Wanda Bryant, Guangming Li, David Martinelli, and Kathryn Vaughn, 'Demystifying and Classifying Electronic Music Instruments', in *Selected Reports in Ethnomusicology*, vol. VIII: *Issues in Organology* (Los Angeles, CA, 1990), p. 41.

2 Thomas Hauser, *Thomas Hauser on Boxing: Another Year Inside the Sweet Science* (Fayetteville, AR, 2014), p. 122.

3 Ian Penman, 'On the Mic: How Amplification Changed the Voice for Good', in *Under-currents: The Hidden Wiring of Modern Music*, ed. Rob Young (New York, 2002), p. 26.

4 Ibid.

5 Michelangelo Antonioni's film *Blow Up* and Francis Ford Coppola's *The Conversation* are films whose narratives centre on the idea of seeing and hearing 'too much'.

6 Juan G. Roederer, *Introduction to the Physics and Psychophysics of Music* (New York, 1975), pp. 26–7.

7 Hugh Robjohns, 'A Brief History of Microphones', www.microphone-data.com, accessed 2016.

8 Garrett Haines, 'Microphones: The Decca Tree Technique', http://tapeop.com, 2005.

9 Karlheinz Stockhausen, *Stockhausen on Music: Lectures and Interviews*, ed. Robin Maconie (London, 1989), p. 77.

10 Ibid, p. 87.

11 Robert Ashley, 'Cut and Splice 2005', www.bbc.co.uk, 2005.

12 Ibid.

13 Ibid.

14 Steve Reich, 'On Pendulum Music', in www.furious.com, 2001.

15 Ibid.

16 John Eaton, 'History of Brainwave Music', http://joeleaton.co.uk, 2016.

17 Alvin Lucier, 'I am Sitting in a Room', www.ubu.com, 2001.

18 Alvin Lucier, 'My Affairs with Feedback', mikroton.net, 2016.

19 'How we made Laurie Anderson's O Superman', Interview with Dave Simpson, www.theguardian.com, 19 April 2016.

20 Dave Tompkins, *How to Wreck a Nice Beach: The Vocoder from World War II to Hip-hop* (New York, 2010), pp. 255–6.

21 R. Murray Schafer, *The Tuning of the World* (New York, 1977), pp. 9–10.

22 In the documentary film *Listen* (2003), Cage asks that we 'let sounds be sounds', and not keep trying to make them mean something.

23 Francisco López, liner notes of *La Selva: Sound Environments from a Neotropical rain Forest*, V2 Records, 1998.

24 Ibid.

25 Ibid.

26 Ibid.

5 Computers

1 Lejaren Hiller and Leonard Issacson, *Experimental Music: Composition with an Electronic Computer* (New York, 1959), p. 2.

2 Counterpoint is the systematic study of voice-leading which is the combination of horizontal and linear consonance and dissonance.

3 Hiller and Issacson, *Experimental Music*, p. 4.

4 Iannis Xenakis, *Formalized Music: Thought in Mathematics and Composition*, Revised Edition (Stuyvesant, NY, 1992), p. ix.

5 Ibid.

6 Milton Babbitt, 'Who Cares if You Listen?', in *Contemporary Composers on Contemporary Music*, ed. Elliott Schwartz and Barney Childs (New York, 1967), p. 247.

7 John Cage, *Silence: Lectures and Writings* (Middletown, CT, 1973), p. 10.

8 Edgard Varèse, 'The Liberation of Sound', *Perspectives of New Music*, V/1 (Autumn–Winter 1966), p. 17. Wronsky (1778–1853) was a Polish philosopher and mathematician.

9 Xenakis, *Formalized Music*, p. 8.

10 Ibid., p. 9.

11 Milton Babbitt, 'An Introduction to the R.C.A. Synthesizer', *Journal of Music Theory*, VIII/2 (Winter 1964), pp. 251–2.

12 James Tenney, quoted in *Mainframe Experimentalism: Early Computing and the Foundations of the Digital Arts*, ed. Hannah Higgins and Douglas Kahn (Berkeley, CA, 2012), p. 138.

13 Hubert Howe, personal communication with the composer, September 2016.

14 Ibid.

15 Hubert Howe, *Electronic Music Synthesis: Controls, Facilities, Techniques* (New York, 1975), p. 176.

16 J. K. Randall, 'Three Lectures to Scientists', *Perspectives of New Music*, V/2 (Spring–Summer 1967), p. 137.

17 J. K. Randall, liner notes on Vanguard Recording VCS 10057.

18 Ibid.

19 Paul Lansky, http://ycpanel.princeton.edu, 2015.

20 Curtis Roads, 'Interview with Paul Lansky', *Computer Music Journal*, XII/3 (Autumn 1983), p. 17.

21 Ibid., p. 18.

22 Joshua Cody, 'An Interview with Paul Lansky', *Computer Music Journal*, XX/1 (Spring 1996), p. 20.

23 The English band Radiohead used a sample for Lansky's piece on their album *Kid A*, having found a used copy in a record store.

24 John Chowing, Liner notes on Wergo CD wer2012-50, 1988.

25 Xenakis, *Formalized Music*, p. 43.

26 Curtis Roads, 'Granular Synthesis of Sound', in *Foundations of Computer Music* (Cambridge, MA, 1987), pp. 150–51.

27 Gary Langan, 'Interview with Gary Langan of the Art of Noise', www.electricity-club.co.uk, 2015.

28 DJ Pierre, 'The Story of Acid House: As Told by DJ Pierre', http://daily.redbullmusicacademy.com, 2012.

29 Ibid.

30 Ikaturo Kakehashi, *I Believe in Music* (Milwaukee, WI, 2002), p. 33.

31 Jonas Wårstad, 'Warren Cann interviewed by Jonas Wårstad', www.discog.info/ultravox-interview5.html, 2015.

32 Phil Collins, 'Classic Tracks: Phil Collins, "In the Air Tonight"', www.mixonline.com, 2015.

33 Simon Trask, 'Future Shock' (interview with Juan Atkins), www.mobeus.org, 1988.

34 Juan Atkins, quoted in Ben Beaumont-Thomas, 'The Roland TR-808: The Drum Machine that Revolutionized Music', www.theguardian.com, 2014.

35 Jahtari, 'The Digital Revolution', www.jahtari.org, 2015.

36 Hancock was no stranger to technology, having played a Fender Rhodes in Miles Davis's band. He had incorporated an analog synthesizer – played by Dr Patrick Gleason – in his own band for his 1973 album *Sextant*. It figures prominently and fascinatingly in the music, but the record sold poorly.

37 S. H. Fernando Jr, 'How Herbie Hancock Crafted a Hip-hop Classic', https://medium.com/cuepoint, 2015.

38 Juno Plus, 'Real Time: An Interview with Roger Linn', www.junodownload.com/plus, 2016.

39 DJ Shadow, *Keyboard Magazine* (October 1997), n.p.

40 Kylee Swenson, www.futureproducers.com, 2006.

41 Tom Bateman, 'How MIDI Changed the World of Music', www.bbc.com, 2012.

42 The MIDI Association, 'MIDI History', www.midi.org, 2015.

43 Bateman, 'How MIDI changed the World of Music'.
44 Sami Yenigun, 'The MIDI Revolution: Synthesizing Music for the Masses', 12 May 2013, www.npr.org.
45 Tom Jenkinson, interview from the film *Modulations* (1998).
46 Paul Tingen, 'Interview with Squarepusher', www.soundonsound. com, 2011.
47 Jeff Parker, 'George Lewis', *BOMB*, XCIII (Autumn 2005), p. 86.
48 Miller Puckette, 'Max at Seventeen', *Computer Music Journal*, XXVI/4 (Winter 2002), p. 35.
49 Pauline Oliveros, 'The Expanded Instrument System (EIS): An Introduction and Brief History', http://deeplistening.org, 2016.
50 Nick Rothwell, 'Max for Live', www.soundonsound.com, 2010.
51 Eivind Aarset, artist page, www.ableton.com, 2016.
52 N. Katherine Hayles, 'Cybernetics', in *Critical Terms for Media Studies*, ed. W.J.T. Mitchell and Mark B. N. Hansen (Chicago, IL, 2010), p. 148.

Epilogue

1 Robert Partridge, 'Why I Killed the King: An Interview with Robert Fripp', *Melody Maker* (5 October 1974), p. 15.
2 Emmanuelle Loubet and Marc Couroux, 'Laptop Performers, Compact Disc Designers, and No-beat Techno Artists in Japan: Music from Nowhere', *Computer Music Journal*, XXIV/4 (Winter 2000), pp. 21–2.

BIBLIOGRAPHY

Adorno, Theodor, 'On Popular Music', in *Essays on Music*, trans. Susan
    H. Gillespie (Berkeley, CA, 2002), pp. 437–69
Ansell, Kenneth, 'Annette Peacock', *Impetus*, VIII (1978), pp. 324–9
Attali, Jacques, *Noise: The Political Economy of Music*, trans. Brian
    Masumi (Minneapolis, MN, 1985)
Babbitt, Milton, 'An Introduction to the R.C.A. Synthesizer', *Journal
    of Music Theory*, VIII/2 (1964), pp. 251–65
——, 'Who Cares if You Listen?', in *Contemporary Composers on
    Contemporary Music*, ed. Elliott Schwartz and Barney Childs
    (New York, 1998), pp. 243–50
Bakan, Michael, et al., 'Demystifying and Classifying Electronic Music
    Instruments', in *Selected Reports in Ethnomusicology*, vol. VIII: *Issues
    in Organology* (Los Angeles, CA, 1990), pp. 37–66
Bangs, Lester, *Psychotic Reactions and Carburetor Dung* (New York, 1987)
Barthes, Roland, 'The Grain of the Voice', in *Image-Music-Text*, trans.
    Stephen Heath (London, 1977), pp. 179–89
Benjamin, Walter, 'The Work of Art in the Age of Mechanical
    Reproduction', in *Illuminations*, ed. Hannah Arendt, trans. Harry
    Zohn (New York, 1968), pp. 217–52
Bennet, Stuart, *A History of Control Engineering, 1800–1930* (London,
    1986)
Benoliel, Bernard, 'Oldfield: With and Without Bedford', *Tempo*, New
    Series, CXX (March 1977)
Bernstein, David, ed., *The San Francisco Tape Music Center* (Berkeley, CA,
    2008)
Cage, John, *Imaginary Landscape No. 5* (New York, 1951)
——, *Silence: Lectures and Writings* (Middletown, CT, 1973)
Cody, Joshua, 'An Interview with Paul Lansky', *Computer Music Journal*,
    XX/1 (1996), pp. 19–24

Eimert, Herbert, *Electronic Music*, trans. D. A. Sinclair (Ottawa, 1954)

Emerson, Keith, *The Art of Electronic Music*, ed. Greg Armbruster (New York, 1984)

Gluck, Bob, *The Miles Davis Lost Quintet and Other Revolutionary Ensembles* (Chicago, IL, 2016)

Goldberg, David Albert Mhadi, 'The Scratch is Hip-hop: Appropriating the Phonographic Medium', in *Appropriating Technology: Vernacular Science and Social Power* (Minneapolis, MN, 2004), pp. 107–44

Gould, Glenn, 'The Prospects of Recording', *High Fidelity Magazine*, XVI/4 (1966), pp. 46–63

Grandmaster Flash with David Ritz, *The Adventures of Grandmaster Flash: My Life, My Beats* (New York, 2008)

Hartsock, Ralph, and Carl Rahkonen, *Vladimir Ussachevsky: A Bio-bibliography* (Westport, CT, 2000)

Hauser, Thomas, *Thomas Hauser on Boxing: Another Year Inside the Sweet Science* (Fayetteville, NC, 2014)

Hayles, N. Katherine. 'Cybernetics', in *Critical Terms for Media Studies*, ed. W.J.T. Mitchell and Mark B. N. Hansen (Chicago, IL, 2010), pp. 145–56

Heckman, Don, 'Jazz-rock', *Stereo Review*, XXXIII/5 (1974)

Higgins, Hannah, and Douglas Kahn, eds, *Mainframe Experimentalism: Early Computing and the Foundations of the Digital Arts* (Berkeley, CA, 2012)

Hiller, Lejaren, and Leonard Issacson, *Experimental Music: Composition with an Electronic Computer* (New York, 1959)

Hopkins, Bill, 'Stockhausen and Others', *Tempo*, New Series, XCVIII (1972), pp. 32–4

Howe, Hubert, *Electronic Music Synthesis: Controls, Facilities, Techniques* (New York, 1975)

Kakehashi, Ikaturo, *I Believe in Music* (Milwaukee, WI, 2002)

King, Michael, *Wrong Movements: A Robert Wyatt History* (Wembley, 1994)

Kostelanetz, Richard, 'John Cage and Richard Kostelanetz: A Conversation About Radio', *Musical Quarterly*, LXXII/2 (1986), pp. 216–27

Lissa, Zofia, Eugenia Tanska and Eugenia Tarska, 'On the Evolution of Musical Perception', *Journal of Aesthetics and Art Criticism*, XXIV/2 (1965), pp. 273–86

Loubet, Emmanuelle, and Marc Couroux, 'Laptop Performers, Compact Disc Designers, and No-beat Techno Artists in Japan: Music from Nowhere', *Computer Music Journal*, XXIV/4 (2000), pp. 19–32

Luening, Otto, 'An Unfinished History of Electronic Music', *Music Educators Journal*, LX/3 (1968), pp. 42–9, 135–42, 145

Lydon, Michael, *Boogie Lightning: How Music Became Electric* (New York, 1980)

Marles, William, 'Duration and Frequency Alteration', *Journal of the Audio Engineering Society*, XIV/2 (1966), pp. 132–9

Martin, George, with Jeremy Hornsby, *All You Need is Ears* (New York, 1979)

Miles, Barry, *Paul McCartney: Many Years From Now* (New York, 1997)

Mitchell, William J., *The Reconfigured Eye* (Cambridge, 1992)

Mullin, Jack, 'Discovering Magnetic Tape', *Broadcast Engineering*, XXI (1979), pp. 80–81

Newman, Richard, *The Making of Mike Oldfield's Tubular Bells* (Cambridge, 1993)

Nin, Anaïs, *The Diary of Anais Nin*, vol. VI (New York, 2012)

Nyman, Michael, *Experimental Music: Cage and Beyond* (New York, 1974)

Ogden, Frank, and Ray Carter, 'The Country Life', *Studio Sound*, XVIII/10 (October 1976), pp. 38–40

Oliveros, Pauline, 'Some Sound Observations', in *Audio Culture: Readings in Modern Music* (New York, 2004, revd edn 2017)

Parker, Jeff, 'George Lewis', BOMB, XCIII (2005)

Partridge, Robert, 'Why I Killed the King: An Interview with Robert Fripp', *Melody Maker* (5 October 1974), pp. 14–15

Passman, Arnie, 'Such Sweet Thunder: Charlie Butten and His Earthy Sound System', *Rolling Stone*, XC (1971), pp. 38, 40

Penman, Ian, 'On the Mic: How Amplification Changed the Voice for Good', in *Under-currents: The Hidden Wiring of Modern Music*, ed. Rob Young (New York, 2002)

Peters, John Durham, 'Helmholtz, Edison, and Sound Theory', in *Memory Bytes: History, Technology, and Digital Culture*, ed. Laren Rabinovitz and Abraham Geil (Durham, 2004)

Pinch, Trevor and Frank Trocco, *Analog Days: The Invention and Impact of the Moog Synthesizer* (Cambridge, 2002)

Poullin, Jacques, 'The Application of Recording Techniques to the Production of New Musical Materials and Forms Applications to Musique Concrète', trans. D. A. Sinclair (Ottawa, 1957)

Prendergast, Mark, 'Tangerine Dream: Changing Use of Technology, Part 1: 1967–1977', *Sound on Sound* (December 1994), pp. 88–94

Puckette, Miller, 'Max at Seventeen', *Computer Music Journal*, XXVI/4 (2002), pp. 31–43

Radigue, Eliane, 'The Mysterious Power of the Infinitesimal', *Leonardo Music Journal*, XIX (2009), pp. 47–9

Randall, J. K., 'Three Lectures to Scientists', *Perspectives of New Music*,
     v/2 (1967), pp. 124–40

Roads, Curtis, 'Granular Synthesis of Sound', in *Foundations of Computer
     Music* (Cambridge, 1987), pp. 145–59

——, 'Interview with Paul Lansky', *Computer Music Journal*, vii/3 (1983),
     pp. 16–24

Roederer, Juan G., *Introduction to the Physics and Psychophysics of Music*
     (New York, 1975)

Schaeffer, Pierre, *In Search of a Concrete Music*, trans. Christine North
     and John Dack (Berkeley, ca, 2012)

Schafer, R. Murray, *The Tuning of the World* (New York, 1977)

Sheff, David, *All We are Saying* (New York, 2000)

Shusterman, Richard, 'The Fine Art of Rap', *New Literary History*, xxii/3
     (1991), pp. 613–32

Smalley, Roger, Review of 'Avant-garde 3', *Musical Times*, cxii/1540
     (1971), p. 567

Stockfelt, Ola, 'Adequate Modes of Listening', in *Keeping Score: Music,
     Disciplinarity, Culture* (Charlottesville, va, 1997)

Stockhausen, Karlheinz, *Stockhausen on Music: Lectures and Interviews*,
     ed. Robin Maconie (London, 1989)

Strange, Allen, *Electronic Music: Synthesis, Techniques, Controls*
     (Dubuque, ia, 1983)

Tannenbaum, Rob, 'A Meeting of Sound Minds: John Cage and Brian
     Eno', *Musician*, lxxxiii (1985), pp. 64–70, 72, 706

Toop, Richard, 'Stockhausen and the Sine-wave: The Story of an
     Ambiguous Relationship', *Musical Quarterly*, lxv/3 (1979)

Varèse, Edgard, and Chou Wen-chung, 'The Liberation of Sound',
     Perspectives of New Music, v/1 (1966)

Vinton, John, ed., *Dictionary of Contemporary Music* (New York, 1971)

Wallach, Jeremy, 'The Poetics of Electrosonic Presence: Recorded Music
     and the Materiality of Sound', *Journal of Popular Music Studies*, xv/2
     (2003), pp. 34–64

Warner, Daniel, and Christoph Cox, *Audio Culture: Readings in Modern
     Music* (New York, 2004)

Watson, Ben, *Frank Zappa: The Negative Dialectics of Poodle Play* (New
     York, 1995)

Xenakis, Iannis, *Formalized Music: Thought in Mathematics and
     Composition*, revd edn (New York, 1992)

ACKNOWLEDGEMENTS

Thanks to:

My father, for teaching me to always read the instructions and always
finish a project.
My colleagues in the Sound Studies Group at Aarhus University,
Denmark, where I began work on this book: Steen Kaargaard
Nielsen, Anette Vandsø, Mads Krogh, Charlotte Rørdam Larsen
and Pia Rasmussen.
Christoph Cox, for his friendship and collaboration with me on our
book *Audio Culture*.
My Five-College composer colleagues, Donald Wheelock, Lewis
Spratlan, Ronald Perera and Charles Bestor, for their many years
of support and friendship.
Marty Ehrlich and Margaux Edwards, my friends and colleagues
at Hampshire College, for sharing with me their great talents
as performers and composers.
Bert A. Anderson, my first electronic music teacher.
Milton Babbitt and J. K. Randall, who lived without compromise the
idea that it is imperative to think deeply about music.
Ben Hayes, Commissioning Editor at Reaktion Books, who suggested
that I write this book, and for his intellectual companionship
throughout the project.
Mary Russo – most of all – for everything.

PHOTO ACKNOWLEDGEMENTS

The author and the publishers wish to thank the below sources of illustrative material and/or permission to reproduce it:

David Corio/Michael Ochs Archives/Getty Images: p. 88; GAB Archive/ Redferns: p. 54; Herve GLOAGUEN/Gamma-Rapho via Getty Images: p. 16; Lynn Goldsmith/Corbis/VCG via Getty Images: p. 110; Chris McKay/Getty Images: p. 130; Zooner GmbH/Alamy Stock Photo: p. 6.

INDEX

Page numbers in *italic* refer to illustrations

Aarset, Eivind 168–9
Ableton Live 166
acid house 151
additive synthesis 58
adequate listening 15
Adorno, Theodor 42
ADSR 67
Akai MP-60 160–61
algorithmic composition 133
Ampex 200A 19
amplification 81
analogue synthesizer 64–7
Anderson, Laurie 110
    voice processing 125
Arfib, Daniel
    Le Souffle du doux (The Whistle
        of the Gentle) 147
    waveshaping 147
ARP 2500 78
ARP 2600 77–8
Ashley, Robert 120–21
Atkins, Juan 156–7
Attali, Jacques 8, 95
audiophiles 19
Augustine, St 42
    San Francisco Tape Music
        Center 33
    The Wolfman 120–21

Babbitt, Milton
    Columbia-Princeton Electronic
        Music Center 33
    Composition for Synthesizer 62
    RCA Synthesizer 11, 136
    'Who Cares if You Listen?' 134
Bambaataa, Afrika *88*
    Planet Rock 155
    turntablism 93
Barron, Bebe and Louis
    circuits 56–7
    Forbidden Planet 8
Barthes, Roland 104
Barton, Todd 75
Beatles, the 47–8
    'Being for the Benefit of
        Mr Kite' 48
    'I Feel Fine' 84–5
    Mellotron 35–6
    'Revolution 9' 48
    'Strawberry Fields Forever'
        35–6, 47–8
Bell, Alexander Graham 115
Bell Labs 137–9
Belleville Three 155–6
Benjamin, Walter 7, 101
Bley, Paul and Annette Peacock
    70–71
Blondie 154

Bode, Harald 60, 84
Boulanger, Nadia 20
Boulez, Pierre 24–5, 147
Bowie, David 13
broadcast profanity delay 39
Bryars, Gavin
    1,2, 1-2-3-4 45–6
    electronic process piece 45
Buchla, Donald
    Buchla Box 64
    sequencer 73
    touch keyboard 72
    voltage control 64
Burke, Edmund 8
Butler, Samuel 43
Butten, Charlie 85

Cage, John 16
    4'33" 126
    Imaginary Landscape No. 1
        55–6, 89–90
    Imaginary Landscape No. 5 32
    Switched-on Bach 68
    Well-tempered Synthesizer 68
Campbell, Clive (DJ Kool Herc)
    91, 94
Carlos, Wendy 54
    Columbia-Princeton Electronic
        Music Center 34
Chamberlin, Harry 35
Childs, Barney 11
Chowning, John
    frequency modulation
        synthesis 144–5
    Stria 145
    Yamaha DX7 145–6
Clapton, Eric 85
Cologne studio 58–9
Columbia-Princeton Electronic
    Music Center 33–4, 61–2
compression 106

Corbett, John 97–8
Corea, Chick 40
Crosby, Bing 19, 112

Davis, Miles
    Bitches Brew 83
    In a Silent Way 49–50, 83
    Kind of Blue 50
    Live at Fillmore 82–3
    Miles in the Sky 81
    On the Corner 83
    Wurlitzer electric piano
        81
De Forest, Lee 57, 83
Decca tree 117
Deleuze, Gilles 8
Deutsch, Herbert 63
digital black 106
drum machine 151–7
dubplating 91–2
Duchamp, Marcel 170–71

ear 113–14
Echoplex 40
Edison, Thomas 115
EDM 165
Eimert, Herbert 11, 59
electric piano 81
electronic process piece 45
Emerson, Keith 69–70
EMS VCS-3 synthesizer 13
Eno, Brian
    Fear of Music 13
    Low 13
    Music for Airports 2/1 44
    tape loop 44–5
envelope generator 67
Eurythmics, the 163

Fairlight CMI synthesizer
    Art of Noise 148–9

Peter Gabriel 148
Trevor Horn 148
feedback 80–86
Ferrari, Luc
    anecdotal music 31, 126
    GRMC 28
    *Presque rien No. 1: Le Lever
        du jour au bord de la mer*
        (Almost Nothing: Dawn
        at the Seaside) 28–31, 127
filters 65–6
flanging 44
Flash, Grandmaster
    turntablism 93
    'The Adventures of
        Grandmaster Flash on
        the Wheels of Steel' 96–7
Fourier, Joseph 57–8
Fripp, Robert 12, 170
Futurists 55

Genesis 36
Goldberg, David Albert Mhadi
    94
Gould, Glenn 68, 102–3
granular synthesis 27, 146
Groupe de Recherches de
    Musique Concrète (GRMC) 25

Hammond B-3 organ 9, 81
Hancock, Herbie 81, 159
Harvey, Jonathan
Hayles, N. Katherine 169
    IRCAM 147
    Mortuos Plango, Vivos Voco
        147–8
Hendrix, Jimi
    Are You Experienced? 101
    Axis: Bold as Love 44
    feedback 101
Henke, Robert 168

Henry, Pierre
    collaborations with Schaeffer
        21
    GRMC 27
    Haut-voltage (High Voltage)
        28
    Le Microphone bien tempéré
        (The Well-tempered
        Microphone) 28
    Le Reine verte (The Green
        Queen) 28
    Le Voyage (The Voyage) 28
    Symphonie pour un homme seul
        (Symphony for a Lone Man)
        24–5
    *Variations pour une porte et un
        soupir* (Variations on a Door
        and a Sigh) 28
Herndon, Holly 131
    MIDI composition 164
high-frequency biasing 19
Hiller, Lejaren
    counterpoint rules 131–2
    Illiac Suite 132–3
    Markov chain 133
Howe, Hubert 140–41

I. G. Farben (BASF) 18
Intonarumori (Noise Machines)
    55

Jammy, King 158–9
Jarre, Jean-Michel 76
Jeck, Phillip
    Vinyl Coda I–III 100
    Vinyl Requiem 99
Jefferson, Marshall 151

Kakehashi, Ikutaro 152–3, 161–2
Kikumoto, Tadao 150
King Crimson 36, 170

Kraftwerk 80
Kramer, Eddie 44

Lansky, Paul
    Mild und Leise 142–3
    Music 360 143
    speech synthesis 143
Leedy, Douglas
    Entropical Paradise 74–5
    self-generating patch 75
Lennon, John 35–6
Lewis, George 166
Linn LM-1 drum machine 157–8
Linn, Roger 160
Lissa, Zofia 14
López, Francisco
    *La Selva: Sound Environments
        from a Neotropical Rain
        Forest* 127–9
    profound listening 127
Loube, Emmanuelle 170
Lucier, Alvin
    feedback composition 124–5
    I am Sitting in a Room 105,
        122–4
    Music for Solo Performer 122
Luening, Otto 11, 33, 39
    Columbia-Princeton Electronic
        Music Center 11, 33
    Low-speed 39–40
Lydon, Michael 103–4, 109

McCartney, Paul 36
Macero, Teo 49–50
Magnetophon K1 18
Marclay, Christian
    Ghost (I Don't Live Today) 99
    Groove 98
    One Thousand Cycles 98
    Record Without a Cover 98
Marshall, Jim 85

Martin, George 35–6, 47–8
Mathews, Max
    Bell Labs 137
    GROOVE system 139
    Music N 137–8, 147–8
    MAX/MSP 148, 166–9
Mellotron 35–6
Melochord 60
Messiaen, Olivier 25–6
Meyer-Eppler 59
microphone types 116
MIDI 161–5
Mitchell, William J. 17–18
Moody Blues
    Days of Future Passed 36
    Mellotron 36
Moog, Robert 62, 67, 70, 79, 84
    Minimoog 76–7
    synthesizer 63
    Theremin 62
Moore, Scotty 12
Moroder, Giorgio 80
Mullin, Jack 19
multi-track tape recorder 38

noise 65
Nyman, Michael 45

Oberheim drum machines
    159
Oldfield, Mike
    multi-tracking techniques
    Tubular Bells 50–52
Oliveros, Pauline
    I of IV 74
    Alien Bog 74
    Buchla 100 synthesizer 73–4
    Bye Bye Butterfly 40
    Expanded Instrument System
        167–8
    heterodyning 74

San Francisco Tape Music
Center 11
tape delay system 40
Olson, Harry F. 61
Orb, The 163–4

Paul, Les 38
pedalboard 12
Penman, Ian 112–13
Perry, Lee 'Scratch' 52
Peters, John Durham 108
Phillips, Sam 12
Phuture 150–51
PPG WAVE synthesizer 148
Princeton University 140–44
proximity effect 117
Puckette, Miller 166–7
Pure Data 148

Radigue, Eliane
ARP 2500 78
Trilogie de la mort (Trilogy on
Death) 78
Randall, J. K.
Music IV and Music IVbf
140–41
Lyric Variations for Violin and
Computer 140–42
Ray Butts EchoSonic 12
RCA Synthesizer 11, 61–2
Reaktor 148
Reed, Lou 85–7
Reich, Steve
Come Out 43
It's Gonna Rain 43
Pendulum Music 121–2
San Francisco Tape Music
Center 33
tape loop 43–4
Reis, Johann 114–15
repetition 41–3

Rhodes electric piano
Miles Davis 82
Chick Corea 82
Rhodes, Harold 81–2
ribbon controller 66–7
Riley, Terry
A Rainbow in Curved Air 80
San Francisco Tape Music
Center 33
ring modulator 40, 66
Risset, Jean-Claude
Bell Labs 139
Mutations 139
Roads, Curtis 146
Rockmore, Clara 63
Roland Corporation
CR-78 153–4
TR-77 153
TB-303 149–51
TR-808 154–7
TR-909 159
room tone 104–5
Run DMC 159

sampler 157–61
San Francisco Tape Music Center
32–3
Schaeffer, Pierre
acousmatic listening 127–8
anamorphosis 90
Concert de bruits (Concert of
Noises) 24
Étude aux chemins de fer
(Railway Study) 22–3
Étude pathétique (Study on Pots
and Pans) 24
Étude violette (Violet Etude) 24
GRMC 25
Morphophone 38
musical notation 51
musique concrète 11, 20–24

Phonogène 35, 37
Quatre Études de bruits (Four Noise Studies) 23
Symphonie pour un homme seul (Symphony for a Lone Man) 24–5
Three-head Tape Recorder 38
turntables 34
Schafer, R. Murray
  keynote sound 125
  signals 125
  soundmark 125–6
  soundscape 125
  The Tuning of the World 126
sel-sync (selective synchronous) recording 38
self-generating patch 75
Sender, Ramon 32–3, 64
sequencer 73, 79
Shadow, DJ 161
Shusterman, Richard 95
Sinatra, Frank 112
Smith, Dave 161–2
Spiegel, Laurie
  Appalachian Grove 139
  Bell Labs 139
  Kepler's Harmony of the Worlds 139
Springer machine 37
Squarepusher 165
standing waves 105
Stockfelt, Ola 15
Stockhausen, Karlheinz
  Electronic Study Nos. 1–2 59
  elektronische Musik 58
  Gesang der Jünglinge 60
  Hymnen 37
  Konkrete Etüde 26, 58
  Kontakte 8, 60
  letter to Karel Goeyvaerts 58–9

live mixing 12
Mikrophonie I 118–20
Subotnick, Morton
  Buchla synthesizer 64
  San Francisco Tape Music Center 33
  sequencer 73
  Silver Apples of the Moon 72
  tape music 11
Sun Ra
  Minimoog 77
  My Brother the Wind 77
SuperCollider 148

Talking Heads 13
Tangerine Dream 36, 79–80
tape delay 39
tape loop 41–5
tape music 11, 32–4
Technics SL-1200MK2 turntable 92–3
technology 9–10
Teitelbaum, Richard
  In-tune 122–3
  Moog synthesizer 123
Tenney, James
  Bell Labs 138–9
  Analog No. 1: Noise Study 138–9
Theodor, Grand Wizard 93
Theremin, Léon 62–3
Trautonium 60
Tubby, King 52, 158
TUBS system 155
turntablist techniques 93–7, 111

Ultravox 153–4
Ussachevsky, Vladimir
  ADSR 67
  Columbia-Princeton Electronic Music Center 11, 33

Sonic Contours 39
tape loop 39

vcs-3 synthesizer 76
Varèse, Edgard
    Columbia-Princeton Electronic
        Music Center 34
    Déserts 26
    Ionisation 55
    lectures on electronic music
        9, 26, 134–5
    Poème électronique 26–7
voltage control 63
voltage controlled amplifier
    67

Wallace, Roy 116
waveforms 65
waveshaping synthesis 146–7
Weber, Walter 18
Weiner, Norbert 56
Wente, E. C. 115
White, Miles 93

Winham, Godfrey 140
Wyatt, Robert
    Immediate Curtain 36
    Mellotron 36

Xenakis, Iannis
    Concret P-H 27
    Formalized Music 133
    GRMC 26
    Mycenae Alpha 135–6
    stochastic music 135
    UPIC system 135
    *Voyage absolu des Unari vers
        Andromède* 136

Zappa, Frank
    Studio Z 46
    tape composition 12–13
    Uncle Meat 46–7
Zawinul, Joe 77–8
Zicarelli, David 168
Zinovieff, Peter 76
Zouk music 52